BACK TO BASICS

U.S.-Iraq Security Cooperation in the Post-Combat Era

Michael Knights and Alex Almeida

ROWMAN &
LITTLEFIELD

Published in association with The Washington Institute for Near East Policy

Published by Rowman & Littlefield
An imprint of The Rowman & Littlefield Publishing Group, Inc.
4501 Forbes Boulevard, Suite 200, Lanham, MD 20706
www.rowman.com

86-90 Paul Street, London EC2A 4NE

©2023 by The Washington Institute for Near East Policy

All rights reserved. No part of this book may be reproduced in any form or by any electronic or mechanical means, including information storage and retrieval systems, without written permission from the publisher, except by a reviewer, who may quote passages in a review.

British Library Cataloguing-in-Publication Information available

Library of Congress Cataloging-in-Publication Data

ISBN 978-1-5381-8301-4 (hardcover)
ISBN 978-1-5381-8302-1 (paperback)
ISBN 978-1-5381-8303-8 (electronic)

∞™ The paper used in this publication meets the minimum requirements of American National Standard for Information Science—Permanence of Paper for Printed Library Materials. ANSI/NISO Z39.48-1992.

The Washington Institute for Near East Policy
1111 19th Street NW, Suite 500
Washington, DC 20036
www.washingtoninstitute.org

Cover photo: Reuters

Contents

List of Illustrations		iv
Acknowledgments		v
Abbreviations		vi
Executive Summary		1
1	The ISF Today: House of Cards, or "Good Enough"?	23
	Leadership: Foundation of Success, Sound Basis for Hope	24
	Force Design and Deployment	29
	Counterterrorism Operations	35
	Level of Iraqi Reliance on U.S.-Led Forces	38
2	The ISF Tomorrow: Where Does It Need to Be?	47
	Job One: No Backsliding	48
	Domestic Primacy, Not Monopoly of Force	49
	Reasonable U.S. Expectations	51
3	Road Map for Future Security Cooperation	55
	Sustain the U.S.-Led Military Safety Net	55
	Transition Some Activities to NATO and Other Partners, 2022–23	60
	Optimize Bilateral U.S.-Iraq Security Cooperation	65
	Principles to Guide Future U.S. Security Cooperation with Iraq	74
	Sketch Out "Plan B" If Normalized Security Cooperation Collapses	78
Annexes		
A	Categories of U.S. Security Cooperation	90
B	Relative Strength of Different ISF Combat Forces	94
	Iraqi Army	94
	Ministry of Interior Federal Police	96
	Ministry of Interior Emergency Response Division	97
	Ministry of Interior Emergency Police/SWAT/Special Tactics	
	Regiment Battalions	98
	Counter Terrorism Service	99
	Iran-Backed (Walai) PMF Line Brigades	100
	Other (Non-Walai) PMF Line Brigades	101
	Overall Comparative Personnel Levels	102
Index		104

List of Illustrations

1.1 ISF Command Table	26
1.2 Iraq Budget Funding for Security Institutions, 2019 and 2021	30
1.3 ISF Personnel	31
1.4 Order of Battle Map	32
1.5 Kurdistan Control Line Map	34
1.6 CJTF-OIR Strike Summary Report	43
2.1 Risk Posed by Iran-Backed Militias to ISF	49
3.1 Iraq's Multinational Security Sector Pantheon	61
3.2 The Security Cooperation Landscape in Iraq	68

Acknowledgments

The authors wish to thank the Washington Institute for Near East Policy for the strong support given to this project, the Institute's Iraq team, and U.S. military missions across the Middle East. In particular, they would like to thank Jill and Jay Bernstein for their unflinching support and encouragement. They would also like to thank the following Institute scholars: Executive Director Robert Satloff, the Howard P. Berkowitz Chair in U.S. Middle East Policy; Research Director Patrick Clawson, the Morningstar Senior Fellow; and Military and Security Studies Program director Michael Eisenstadt, the Khan Fellow. Institute experts, particularly Nathan and Esther K. Wagner Fellow Bilal Wahab, quickly supported this paper with peer reviewing. External peer reviewers cannot be named due to their government positons in the United States, Britain, Iraq, and other coalition nations, but the authors owe them a special debt of gratitude. Finally, thanks go to the wonderful publications team at the Institute, especially Maria Radacsi and Jason Warshof.

Abbreviations

ANSF	Afghan National Security Forces
AUMF	Authorization for the Use of Military Force
CAP	combat air patrol
CJTF-OIR	Combined Joint Task Force–Operation Inherent Resolve
CTEF	Counter-IS Train and Equip Fund
CTF	Centralized Training Facility (Taji, Iraq)
CTS	Counter Terrorism Service (Iraq)
DCS	Direct Commercial Sales
EDA	Excess Defense Articles
EUAM-I	European Union Advisory Mission–Iraq
ESF	Emergency Support Fund
FID	foreign internal defense
FMF	Foreign Military Financing
FMS	Foreign Military Sales
IMET	International Military Training and Education
IS	Islamic State
ISF	Iraqi security forces
ISR	intelligence, surveillance, and reconnaissance
JOC-I	Joint Operations Center–Iraq
JOEP	Jordan Operational Engagement Program
KASOTC	King Abdullah II Special Operations Training Center (Jordan)
KCL	Kurdistan Control Line
KRI	Kurdistan Region of Iraq
NADR	Nonproliferation, Antiterrorism, Demining, and Related (programs)
NMI	NATO Mission Iraq
NSS	National Security Service
OC	Operations Command
ONSA	Office of the National Security Advisor
OSC-I	Office of Security Cooperation–Iraq
PMF	Popular Mobilization Forces
PM-NOC	Prime Minister–National Operations Center
QK	quwat khasa (special forces)
SDF	Syrian Democratic Forces

Executive Summary

On December 31, 2021, the U.S.-led coalition in Iraq will undergo a formal "transition of mission" to a non-combat advise and assist effort. The coalition is essentially already at this stage, but the deadline underlines the change in a way that will hopefully be widely recognized and accepted within Iraq and within Washington. With small adjustments to force posture, one chapter of the U.S.-led security cooperation in Iraq will end and another will begin. This paper imagines what this next chapter can and should look like.

The time to think about this issue is now: even though Combined Joint Task Force–Operation Inherent Resolve (CJTF-OIR, the coalition) may have a couple of years left in Iraq, there needs to be a gentle and orderly off-ramping of today's coalition-led security cooperation into tomorrow's more modest security assistance programs.

The eventual phaseout of CJTF-OIR will be year zero for a new epoch of U.S.-Iraq security cooperation and strategic relations. This era would not be one of invasion and state-building (2003–11), nor of major combat operations to defeat of the Islamic State (2014–20), but rather something new. It would be the inception of a fresh effort, not a contingency operation but a normalized steady state, a regular condition-based sustained partnership without an end point or exit strategy. A purpose-built vision needs to undergird this new era, with a basis not reliant on contingency authorizations, such as the nearly defunct 2002 Authorization for the Use of Military Force in Iraq and the aging post-9/11 AUMF from 2001.

This study comes in response to "demand signals" from both the U.S. Congress and the executive branch. It aims to answer three basic questions: First, how effective are the Iraqi security forces (ISF) today? The collapse in August 2021 of the Afghan National Security Forces (ANSF), which were much less resilient than hoped, necessitates a tough but fair look at the ISF. Second, the study asks how the United States wants and needs the ISF to develop in the coming years in terms of capability and self-reliance. If security cooperation is a journey, what are the milestones? What is the United States trying to achieve in Iraq's security sector, and is it achievable? Third, how should America adjust its security cooperation going forward? The study sketches out a road map for reaching U.S. milestones and near-term objectives in security cooperation with Iraq.

This paper may be accused by some of being too optimistic about the outlook for Iraq and the backdrop for future security cooperation—namely, that moderate political leadership will continue in Iraq's forthcoming 2021–25 term of government, during which period the United States will neither be evicted by a withdrawn letter of invitation nor by unsustainable security risks. Though this outlook can appear, as one reviewer noted, Panglossian (i.e., excessively optimistic), the assessment is based on the authors' detailed observation of the Iraqi scene for a combined three decades. Iraq has made significant progress under capable prime ministers such as Mustafa al-Kadhimi and Haider al-Abadi, and with strong international support. Iraq is still on that path, as indicated by the steep losses for Iran-backed militias in the October 10, 2021, Iraqi elections, when the key Iran-aligned Fatah Alliance dropped from forty-eight seats to just seventeen.

Equally important, the point of departure for this study logically *has* to be continuation of an improving U.S.-Iraq strategic relationship under an effective Iraqi prime minister who is loyal to Iraq. If the U.S. military presence is disinvited from Iraq or intimidated out of Iraq in 2022, the outlook for U.S.-Iraq security cooperation alters so fundamentally, and so negatively, that a study such as this becomes irrelevant until circumstances change. Where this study nods to more negative scenarios, it is to identify practical steps the United States can take to minimize the risk of negative developments and temporarily mitigate their ill effects.

Today's Iraqi Security Forces: Good Enough, and Mostly Self-Reliant

Although the Afghanistan and Iraq conflicts began at almost the same time—and will be forever twinned in many minds—the current U.S. security relationship with Iraq really began in 2014. Today's mission in Iraq is thus not a decades-spanning, trillion-dollar quagmire but instead the Obama, Trump, and Biden administrations' conscious rejection of the transformative nation-building projects of the post-9/11 period. U.S. forces returned to Iraq in 2014 as invited partners, not as uninvited liberators and occupiers. CJTF-OIR deliberately cultivated an Iraqi-led war effort in which Iraqis did the vast majority of the fighting (and dying) and in which the United States avoided the temptation to transform the ISF into a U.S. military clone. The wisdom of that approach is now bearing fruit.

Today, the ISF is consolidating its success against the Islamic State (IS). Operating in tiny groups, the terrorist group is not able to control populated places during daylight hours, its activities inside Iraq's cities are extremely subdued, and it has almost ceased mounting external operations against the U.S. homeland and persons. Next, the ISF needs to secure Iraq's borders to prevent IS from bringing veteran reinforcements and newly adolescent IS fighters from the al-Hawl camp in Syria and from Turkey. New IS recruiting must not benefit from the long-term garrisoning of Sunni "liberated" areas by primarily Shia militias from other parts of Iraq.

The elimination of the Islamic State's residual cells will be a slow process that relies upon the full spectrum of development and resettlement of civilians, not just upon security operations. The ISF is thus not a force fighting for survival against a powerfully growing enemy—as was the case with the ANSF and the Taliban—but rather a military that has *already* succeeded in its basic mission of containing IS.

Day in, day out, the ISF is whittling away IS with a minimum of U.S. assistance. Since 2014, the ISF—not the U.S.-led coalition—has provided the vast majority of the resources and *all* the ground combat forces in the counter-IS campaign. In 2021, the United States no longer trains any Iraqi tactical units, aside from small programs with the Counter Terrorism Service

(CTS) and other special forces, and requested funding for training declined from $282.8 million in fiscal year 2021 to $20 million in fiscal year 2022.[1] Nor does the U.S. government directly maintain Iraq's equipment now, with fleet-wide maintenance of Iraqi ground vehicles by the U.S. military largely a thing of the past. In the FY2022 requested package for Iraq, the previous year's $24 million budget for spare parts was entirely removed.[2] Sustainment support dropped from $124.2 million in FY2021 to $20 million in the FY2022 request.[3]

Despite a steadily reducing U.S. role, Iraq has learned how to "muddle through" in sustaining its ground forces. U.S. defense contractors have focused their support on aerial platforms, where 82 percent mission availability rates have been sustained in the key systems.[4] Although non-combat provision of U.S. intelligence, surveillance, and reconnaissance (ISR) support remains important, the number of coalition strikes in Iraq is very low (averaging 7.2 per month) and will be phased out from the start of 2022.[5] The ISF is thus not leaning heavily on the U.S.-led coalition, and U.S. touch points with the ISF are limited to the very top (the national command headquarters) and at the sharp end (non-combat support to the special forces, intelligence and air assets that are Iraq's deadliest capabilities).

Job One: No Backsliding

The United States does not need Iraq or its security forces to effect a radical change of trajectory, but rather to make ongoing course corrections and hopefully to sustain an increase in the velocity of reforms. But first, Iraq must not backslide. Post-2003 reconstruction of the ISF has been curtailed multiple times, akin to a man pushing a huge boulder up a hill and failing to push it over the crest, hoping momentum will take it over but instead seeing it roll back over him each time. America has the rare opportunity for a do-over: to not repeat the error of abrupt military withdrawal in 2011.

The 2012–14 period demonstrated how rapidly the ISF can erode over a short period of years. Long-term ISF-watchers know that the problem is not that the ISF has failed to become "good enough" to keep IS at a low level, but rather that it may quickly *cease* to be "good enough" if U.S. assistance is abruptly removed or the military leadership once again is politicized.

The reason is that a deep-seated fragility and a lack of self-confidence exist in the post-2014 ISF, for whom the defeat at Mosul is still fresh. ISF victories were largely won alongside the U.S.-led coalition, and their defeats occurred when the coalition was absent. The potential for backsliding must be especially vivid in the aftermath of the collapse of the ANSF in Kabul, coincident with the withdrawal of U.S. forces. The minimum U.S. objective for the ISF should be no backsliding, either via the politicization of military leadership or the stripping of military budgets to favor militias. Progress in ISF development must be allowed to "set," in the same manner that concrete is left to harden before any supports are removed.

Build an ISF That Can Defeat Its Domestic Adversaries

Many critics of the ISF point to the disconcerting number of anti-American militias that operate within the security forces, both inside the Popular Mobilization Forces (PMF) and other forces to lesser and varying degrees. Yet, different from the case of Lebanese Hezbollah—where the terrorist group has a clear military advantage over forces loyal to the state—the balance of forces is much closer in Iraq and arguably weighted in the state's favor.

Although marbled with militia penetration, the bulk of the ISF *is* still under the control of the Iraqi government and the situation is tenable and improving, not merely salvageable or declining. The question for U.S. policymakers is whether the diversion of some U.S. military aid is a worthwhile price for the maintenance of U.S. influence over the majority of the ISF. Put another way, is denying pro-Iranian groups access to basic weapons and vehicles (or indeed to sanctioned Russian weapons purchases) worth deliberately creating a vacuum in Iraq that Iran and Russia will fill to dominate Iraq's future? The answer is clearly no. Being able to "hang in" and work in such complex and challenging environments is a key test of fitness for America in the forthcoming era of strategic cooperation and so-called gray zone warfare.

U.S. security cooperation should aim to make the disciplined government-controlled ISF units the "first among equals" and, over time, the dominant military power inside Iraq. To encapsulate the new U.S. mission, Washington might draw upon and adapt the U.S. military concept of foreign internal defense, which envisages: "Programs or activities taken by a host nation government to free and protect its society from subversion, lawlessness, insurgency, violent extremism, terrorism and other threats to its security."[6]

These are achievable aims, particularly if undertaken steadily and in a sustained manner. The ISF is outfighting IS on a daily basis across multiple provinces. And loyalist ISF units are going toe-to-toe with militias to contest control of the government center, the International Zone, and economic hubs like airports and border crossings. The results are messy, but ultimately successful, episodes of pushback against militia efforts. Numerous successful arrests of militiamen have been made by praetorian ISF special forces, even if an intimidated and complicit judiciary later released some senior detainees. These indicators show growing confidence and firmness by ISF when it is led well by the prime minister and the command staff.

Identify Reasonable U.S. Conditions for Security Cooperation

Although the United States needs to be pragmatic about Iraq's ability to fix its most vexing problems (such as militias), America should identify some desirable changes in the operating environment for security cooperation in Iraq. America has to play, but it should progressively change the rules of the game. Reasonable U.S. expectations include the following:

- **Reduced security threat to U.S. advisors.** The threat to U.S. and coalition forces in Iraq must reduce reasonably quickly. Continuous downward trending in the number of militia attacks on U.S. and coalition targets should be a prerequisite for the release of premium elements of the security cooperation package.

- **Decreased diversion of U.S. aid.** The risk of diversion of U.S. aid must also reduce very rapidly, and ideally in the 2022 Iraqi budget. In particular, the United States has every right, as the largest security cooperation provider to Iraq, to expect that Iraq's defense and security budget is well managed. Thus, the budgets of the Ministry of Defense and CTS must be protected from predation by other security agencies. In the 2021 budget, for instance, the Defense Ministry suffered a 25.6 percent decrease in its funds and CTS lost 19.9 percent of funding, while the PMF saw a 17 percent increase in its budget.[7] In effect, U.S. security assistance created space for the diversion of Defense Ministry and CTS funding to the PMF, which is absolutely *not* the intended effect of U.S. support. The trend of growing PMF funding at the expense of Defense Ministry and CTS procurement and sustainment needs to stop. The United States and other security assistance providers should condition some aid on the more even distribution of future cuts to defense spending across Iraq's agencies.

- **Improved Baghdad-Kurdistan and intra-Kurdish synergies.** Domestic cooperation and deconfliction between Iraqi agencies (especially with the Peshmerga) must improve meaningfully and within a short timeframe. Iraq and the Kurdistan Region (aka Kurdistan Region of Iraq, or KRI) need to correct multiple gross inefficiencies in federal-Kurdish and intra-Kurdish security arrangements, through ongoing Peshmerga reunification and more effective federal-Kurdish policing of their internal border. The federal-Kurdish revenue-sharing dispute cannot be an open-ended justification for Washington to pay a $20 million-per-month slice of Peshmerga salaries. Comprehensive integration of Kurdistan Region security forces via milestones and measures of progress is a reasonable U.S. expectation.

- **Greater focus on human rights and anti-corruption.** Human rights and anti-corruption concerns must be addressed more seriously. The United States should expect and review measurable progress in

Iraq's weeding out of human rights abusers and corrupt officers from its command cadres.

Such requests might form the basis for loose conditionality on the continuation of *some* U.S. assistance—not holding the entire security cooperation relationship at risk, but perhaps some premium parts of the package (e.g., a portion of funding, or no-cost or low-cost granting of Excess Defense Articles, or sensitive and sought-after technology transfers and intelligence sharing).

Ride Out the Militia Storm in 2022

Iran-backed militias in Iraq will not readily accept an ongoing presence of U.S.-led coalition forces in Iraq in 2022 and beyond. Such militias will probably try to rattle the transitioning Iraqi government—which may still be in caretaker mode following the October 2021 elections—with the threat of violence, and violence itself, to seek an actual drawdown of remaining international advisors.

The U.S. government can and should take some proactive steps to reduce the risk of an eviction crisis. The transition of mission to a "non-combat" operation for all Iraq-based forces should be advertised, and the clearest distinction visible to Iraqis would be the end of all U.S. kinetic operations inside Iraq (i.e., end all U.S. airstrikes, with the exception of self-defense actions).

Sites should not be closed as the footprint of the U.S.-led coalition is now at its irreducible minimum. In terms of raw numbers, the 2,500 U.S. troops in Iraq, plus up to a thousand other coalition forces, represent the minimal viable force size to support a range of U.S. and partner government actions in Iraq. Ahead of December 31, 2021, the United States must make crystal clear to politicians in Baghdad and Washington that a full coalition departure from Iraq would be quite disastrous for the broader international presence within, and international support to, Iraq and Syria. Without the logistics and force protection assets of the coalition, most of which are contributed by America, it would be hard for many entities to remain in Iraq and Syria, notably U.S., European, Asian, and Gulf embassies; NATO and other security cooperation providers; and coalition forces in Syria, where the Islamic State is trying to develop a base to reconstitute its threat to Iraq.

As a symbol of continuity in international support for Iraq, it would seem risky to diminish the coalition's mandate, resources, or profile at a time when Iraqi military confidence has not hardened and when the memory of U.S. withdrawal from Afghanistan is fresh. As long as the Iraqi government continues to extend its invitation to international advisors in 2022–23, the U.S.-led coalition should stay at roughly the current levels (2,500 troops) to signal steadiness and reassurance to Iraq and our coalition partners.

This situation is not a case of leaving U.S. persons in harm's way merely to avoid the inevitable end of a lost cause, as the U.S. government now characterizes Afghanistan, but rather to cement gains in Iraq, where the heavy lifting has been finished and where U.S.-led military support has already helped Iraq *succeed* against the Islamic State. U.S. persons do still face threats in Iraq—there have been two U.S. military deaths and two U.S. citizen contractor deaths in Iraq in the past twenty months[8]—but it is important for U.S. adversaries (from great power competitors to terrorist groups) to understand that they cannot drive America out of strategic relationships by killing American diplomats and trainers. If America is shown to be a "giant with clay feet," it will only encourage more attacks on Americans wherever enemies seek to drive them out.

Start the Transition to NATO Capacity Building

In the 2023–24 timeframe, CJTF-OIR may well have run its course, having demonstrably achieved its mission. At that point, today's mainly-U.S. coalition effort should probably be split across two interconnected lines of effort: bilateral U.S.-Iraq security cooperation and NATO.

Backed by a robust exchange of letters since 2016 with three successive Iraqi prime ministers and North Atlantic Council authorization, NATO Mission Iraq (NMI) is now willing and appropriately authorized to expand its support to the ISF and Iraqi security institutions in the coming years.

(Indeed, NMI now has full diplomatic status, privileges, immunities, and facilities.) NATO currently lacks funding and equipment, both of which the United States is in a position to divest as CJTF-OIR ramps down. Importantly, however, the thirty-nation alliance has access to the large numbers of U.S. and non-U.S. advisors needed to develop long-term, persistent relationships within the Iraqi security ministries and uniformed ISF.

Alongside other non-U.S. "unified action partners"—the European Union Advisory Mission–Iraq (EUAM-I), the UN Development Programme, and individual states—NATO has significant potential to advise at ministerial, secretary general, and chief of defense staff levels, plus their deputies. In the first phase of expanded engagement in 2022, NMI has been invited by Iraq to advise individual service branches (Iraqi Ground Forces Command, Iraqi Air Defense Command, Iraqi Naval Forces Command, Iraqi Air Defense Forces, and Iraqi Army Air Forces Command) within the Defense Ministry, followed by other ministries (Ministry of Interior, in partnership with EUAM-I) and the Ministry of Peshmerga Affairs in the Kurdistan Region.

The U.S and NATO should plan out a slow transition of U.S. personnel and equipment from their present badging under CJTF-OIR to new badging under NMI. Eventually, NMI could take over many of the "care and feeding" and base defense responsibilities that drive up personnel levels at today's CJTF-OIR, initially with almost the same level of U.S. contribution of personnel and funding, but eventually with a more diverse set of contributors. The United States is one of the few nations that could provide sufficient civilian advisors in the midst of a fragile security environment to allow NMI to operate effectively. The United States could ensure its contribution is counted against its contribution to NATO.

NATO capacity-building efforts are exactly what the ISF needs to overcome its observed weaknesses in professionalism, leadership, planning, readiness, and sustainment. In 2016, an operational task force narrowly focused on defeating the Islamic State was ideal for graduating new brigades for urban battles, and the role could not have been undertaken by a small NATO mission. In contrast, the future requirements of the ISF are much more suited to working with small groups of NATO advisors who can help Iraq address any threats to the country's future, not just the Islamic State. For instance, NMI could be effective in the following areas:

- **Force structure planning** will allow Iraq to realize the economies and synergies that it needs to undertake its mission with declining defense and security budgets.

- **Definition of roles and missions** for each security force would bring clarity to resourcing, rightsizing, and deployments.

- **Readiness initiatives** include spare parts inventory and supply chain systems, and readiness and training policies. English language tuition needs to be expanded to cope with the demand of the ISF's technical and procurement branches.

- **Human resource management systems** will ensure that personnel are placed in jobs that match and further develop their skills and experience. NMI can also help Iraq ensure that redundant ISF members (including PMF) are encouraged to separate from the ISF—with vocational training and new business microgrants—into legitimate private-sector occupations as opposed to militia or criminal movements.

Jordan: The Model for U.S.-Iraq Security Cooperation

As NATO takes over some missions, the U.S.-Jordan relationship should be the model for the remaining aspects of bilateral U.S.-Iraq cooperation. As the State Department notes, "Jordan's stability and security are priorities for the United States."[9] Washington is committed to strengthening Jordanian security forces without the identification of any particular enemy against which the support is focused. Exactly this approach should be adopted with Iraq.

Memorialized in a series of nonbinding, multiyear MOUs,[10] U.S. security cooperation is planned out in multiyear blocks, for instance, the intention to provide a minimum of $350 million of Foreign Military Financing (FMF) to Jordan each year.[11] This multiyear approach represents a U.S. commitment to long-term support, which in turn can encourage reform and the cohesive building of capabilities using multi-budget (as opposed to year-on-year) funding. Like Iraq, Jordan is one of the largest global accounts with the FMF and Foreign Military Sales (FMS) systems.[12] Like Iraq, Jordan uses general and country-specific tailored U.S. security cooperation programs (e.g., the $234 million Jordan Border Security Program).[13]

Jordan is a particularly suitable model because some kind of special bilateral arrangement is needed to gently transition Iraq from the massive contingency security cooperation of the counter-IS war to the traditional security cooperation relationship that will exist after 2023, when CJTF-OIR is most likely to expire in Iraq. U.S. funding does not need to match today's Counter-IS Train and Equip Fund (CTEF) dollar for dollar. Iraq should be weaned off CTEF in a gradual way before becoming mainly reliant on traditional security cooperation tools, such as FMF and FMS.

The drop-off could be very steep unless Iraq is helped to adjust. Title 10 (military-administered) support tools such as CTEF make the divestment of equipment quick and flexible, while Title 22 (State Department-administered) traditional tools (like FMS and FMF) are slower and more administratively cumbersome. CTEF needs to be replaced with some kind of Iraq carve-out within a global fund such as Section 333 (Authority to Build Capacity) funding (e.g., the Jordan Operational Engagement Program, or JOEP)[14] or via a country-specific FMF mechanism that emerges as a new section of code in the U.S. defense budget (such as the Jordan Border Security Program).[15] In Iraq's case, for instance, this is an argument for transferring U.S. support to the Ministry of Peshmerga Affairs out of the declining CTEF fund and into a specialized bilateral fund such as Section 333 (Authority to Build Capacity) of the U.S. defense budget.

Develop and Fund a Five- or Ten-Year Security Cooperation Plan

As in Jordan, where multiyear plans underpin the relationship, Iraq and the United States need to begin with a foundational road map that comprises identified destinations, milestones, and waypoints. The longer a joint plan can be, the better for acquisition planning: five years at a minimum, but ideally ten years, to enable efficient long-term planning and budgeting processes. A joint strategic review process at the Prime Minister's Office level needs to lay out a multiyear, multi-budget plan for Iraqi internal defense requirements, including established roles and missions for the different security forces and a force structure review.

This review is vital for a range of reasons.

- First, it will create a baseline for rightsizing and restructuring the ISF so that it better fits the task set and also Iraq's tightening budget resources.

- Second, the identification of roles and missions for all the ISF—including the PMF—is critical for the redeployment of forces and the reduction of duplication of roles (e.g., the redundant layering of army, border, and PMF forces in many areas). In some areas, the need for new or consolidated units may be identified, such as the folding-in of Kurdistan Region units or personnel into Iraqi formations such as CTS or joint commands along the Kurdistan Control Line. For the first time, Iraq will have defined roles and missions (and thus budgeting and deployment guidance) for forces such as the Federal Police and the PMF.

- Third, such a process will make international support easier—for instance, by gaining a clear understanding of how Iraqi ministries share responsibilities for critical infrastructure protection.

Iraq must set aside sufficient funding for agreed projects and meet certain conditions in order to receive the support contained within each part of the security cooperation plan. For instance, Iraq should return Ministry of Defense and CTS funding to higher levels, to reflect the diversion of Defense Ministry and CTS procurement and sustainment funding to the PMF. Iraq must offset this diversion and later apply any cuts to defense spending more evenly. Iraq should also initiate self-funding of some security cooperation efforts as a demonstration of commitment and as part of a partnership funding agreement. This self-funding would ensure that Iraq would be forced to make difficult prioritization decisions.

If Iraq can make such commitments, then not only the United States but also deep-pocketed supporters (like Saudi Arabia and the United Arab Emirates) might be encouraged to make larger and longer-term commitments within the framework of a Security Sector Reform Trust Fund. For instance, Gulf state sponsors might be ideal for undertaking infrastructure development at Iraqi bases and for the divestment of (barely) used military equipment and spare parts. Donations would be pooled, with earmarking of funds to reflect the national interests of donors (women's issues, peace and security, policing, counterterrorism, etc.). The fund would activate projects on the basis of a formula of matching Iraqi and international funding.

Training via Joint Exercises

Finally, as in Jordan, the United States should arrange regular joint exercise programs with Iraq to signal U.S. rotating and nonpermanent presence, but also its enduring relationships, engagement, and commitment. Central Command should develop similar special forces training programs to those that exist with the King Abdullah II Special Operations Training Center in Jordan, potentially in partnership with KASOTC itself, which has a close relationship with Iraq's Ministry of Defense. Central Command could initially hold small special forces and air force training exercises inside Iraq multiple times per year. If carefully built around the adapting threat from IS or other domestic adversaries, such exercises might help Iraq develop counterinsurgency approaches (such as night operations; ambushes; air/artillery and ISR) integration; and support to local special forces, such as local SWAT teams and the commando units of Iraqi brigades and divisions).

Initially, the United States should negotiate access and protections for such exercises on a case-by-case basis. Eventually, if Iraq stabilizes and becomes familiar with a normalized security relationship, it may be possible to develop more formal Status of Forces and Acquisition and Cross-Servicing agreements, and later a structure similar to the 2021 U.S.-Jordan Defense Cooperation Agreement. Optimistically, the United States and Iraq should envision small exercises growing into larger annual exercises and eventually also biennial large-scale exercises that might involve regional states (akin to the U.S.-Egypt Bright Star exercises).

Build Strong, Narrow Bilateral Relationships

With NMI ideally leading on broader security sector reform and professionalization of the entire ISF enterprise, the U.S. bilateral partnership should be parsimonious and focus on building very strong, relatively narrow relationships with certain parts of the ISF. This longevity and focus are how the United States succeeded in inculcating high levels of professionalism in the CTS, by growing the young Iraqi special forces lieutenants of 2004 into the Iraqi colonels of 2021.

U.S. advisors (within coalition, NMI, and bilateral security cooperation organizations) must get out of their secure compounds and into Iraqi ministries and headquarters as often as is practical. Some security risk must be accepted to do this. The aim must be more engagement, with a small footprint and a lowered visual signature, stressing creativity and flexible operations approaches under U.S. chief of mission (ambassadorial) and NATO oversight. Ideally, U.S. advisors should be selected and promoted with consideration for their willingness to serve more than a minimum one-year period in Iraq, to aid relationship building and to ameliorate the cycle of constant one-year reinvention of the wheel without significant incremental progress.

As in the recent U.S. "by, with, and through" operations with the Syrian Democratic Forces (SDF), the United States should supplement an already capable partner with just enough additional capability so that it can defeat current threats, the "tactical advantage" model proposed by Mick Mulroy and Eric Oehlerich.[16] A U.S. replacement for the coalition Special Operations Advisor Group should adopt the same pragmatic approach.[17] While NMI focuses on institution-building, U.S. bilateral assistance should help Iraq build out intelligence-driven, direct-action capabilities in provincial-level police commando and tribal mobilization forces. This assistance will require engagement not only with partners closer to the United States like the Defense Ministry and CTS but also Ministry of Interior elements such as local SWAT teams and intelligence officers, and border enforcement units. Above all, Iraq needs a diamond-hard counter-coup force to defend the government center, built around special operations and armored forces.

Although the United States should, of course, encourage Iraq to operate Iraqi intelligence, surveillance, and reconnaissance and aerial strike capabilities, and the "fusion" cells required to get intelligence to strike aircraft, the United States should not be overly focused on exactly duplicating a U.S.-style ISR and surgical airstrike capability. During planned operations, the U.S. military can continue to supplement Iraqi ISR coverage using assets already committed to the Central Command theater.

More fundamentally, the aspiration of the ISF should not be to answer counterterrorism challenges with airstrikes inside Iraq's own territory: that response is the U.S. approach to foreign counterterrorism, but not to domestic counterterrorism in America, nor a normal end state for any country to aspire to. A more normal aspiration for Iraq will be to achieve sufficient force density to deny IS space to operate, to gain more popular support and intelligence tip-offs from the public, and to have a raiding capacity spread across all the provinces that can execute warrant-based targeting and court systems that can prosecute offenders without fear of intimidation.

Be Ready for the Unthinkable: An Iraqi Eviction of U.S. Forces

The earlier sections have focused on the authors' base case scenario—an Iraq in which moderate political leadership continues in the 2021–25 term of government and in which the United States is neither evicted by a withdrawn invitation nor decides to leave because of unsustainable security risks. So, what if Iraq suffers setbacks that push the country in a different direction?

Iraq could simply disinvite foreign military advisors via a parliamentary vote that could spur a prime minister to rescind the letter of invitation or to make a decision unilateral of parliament. On January 7, 2020, the Iraqi parliament held such a session—albeit without establishing a legal quorum—at which the parties present held a vote to call for the withdrawal of all foreign forces from Iraq. Iran's militia proxies in Iraq continue to call for such a full withdrawal of all foreign forces by January 1, 2022, though today's Iraqi government has made it clear that this is not expected to occur.

It is hard to overstate how devastating such a change in Iraqi government behavior would be for U.S. and international presence in Iraq, and for international support to Iraq (through security cooperation, economic assistance, and investment). The scenario underlines the absolutely pivotal role of the office of prime minister. It can make all the difference between a good U.S.-Iraq relationship and a nonexistent one. Therefore, as an obvious point, the United States should care deeply who Iraq's prime ministers are and should strongly support those premiers who are in favor of continued security cooperation relationship with the U.S.-led coalition.

Post-Afghanistan, there should clearly be a general sharpening of thinking and a review of plans for noncombatant evacuations from Iraq, including eligible Iraqi persons, though the December 31, 2019, crisis at the U.S. embassy in Baghdad demonstrated that the system has been exercised recently and is probably in good shape. Even so, more focus must be directed to the day after such a withdrawal order so that the United States is not confronted by an outcome it has not properly prepared for. Basic questions need answering, such as these: What does the United States do if an

Iran-aligned government is formed under an anti-American prime minister? What steps must America take, immediately and eventually, if the coalition is disinvited? And what should America do if militias cause the U.S.-led coalition significant casualties in one of their attacks?

Prepare a Temporary Plan B

The first and most obvious step for the United States would be to clearly and starkly warn Iraqi political-faction leaders of the risks that may emerge in January 2022 and beyond. U.S. officials should paint a realistic picture of international withdrawal from Iraq, including all its economic and diplomatic second-order impacts.

Washington can help to gather a team of factions that know how to act in the case of a new effort by militias to use parliament to evict foreign forces. Such a bloc could contest any parliamentary vote, as opposed to merely abstaining from it or remaining outside the chamber. If the disinvitation is initiated at the prime ministerial level, such a bloc could marshal a parliamentary vote to demand the continuation of coalition and NATO security cooperation, and could undertake the requisite back-channel talks with all factions, including those who have historically been hostile to the U.S. presence but which may be less so today. At the same time, Washington must remain open to viable partial solutions where they are possible (such as moving some assets to the Kurdistan Region with Iraq's approval).

Under some circumstances, NMI might be able to sustain its mission in Baghdad even after eviction or departure of the U.S. diplomatic and military presence, but it would be a thin reed to depend on. Militia leaders have stated that NATO would also be asked to leave, and NATO would logistically have to depart unless there could be a sudden influx of U.S. personnel and capabilities.

In such a dire scenario, the Kurdistan Region of Iraq would probably be America's least-bad plan B in Iraq. At such a moment, America needs to be tough-minded and stand for U.S. interests and long-term partnerships with the Kurds and Iraqi moderates. The sovereignty of Iraq is clearly a consideration, but so too is the maintenance of strategic outposts (in Syria) and strategic relationships (with Iraqi Kurdistan). If Kadhimi falls and is replaced by a pro-Iranian prime minister, the United States should not hesitate to protect its interests and its partners in Iraq using any combination of expedient measures, because Iraq will have already lost a large measure of its sovereignty to Iran.

The KRI would provide a safer environment in which certain vital aspects of the U.S. mission could be maintained even if federal Iraq became untenable as an operating area for a period of time, though U.S. bases in the KRI would probably face ongoing drone and rocket attacks from pro-Iran elements and Iran itself.

Alongside or as a partial alternative to Kurdistan, Jordan's military bases offer some of the same potential fallback options, especially in regard to supporting the U.S. advisor mission at al-Tanf in Syria or providing a base for U.S. ISR aircraft and U.S. Special Forces training for the ISF, and exercises involving the ISF. Iraqi aircraft could potentially be maintained from Jordan's air bases also. Access agreements should be readied so that such a switch could happen immediately.

All these potential scenarios and their variants should be "gamed out" in classified interagency tabletop exercises. None of these workarounds would be attractive to Iraq's government and military, but Iraq must understand that they would be the remaining options if the United States either cannot or will not remain in federal Iraq. The second-order consequences of a hasty withdrawal of the U.S.-led coalition, particularly if accompanied by an eviction of NATO, need to be clearly understood by Iraqi leaders and politicians well before December 31, 2021. The departure would mean the closure of the U.S. embassy in Baghdad, and potentially other embassies, and the cessation of much of Iraq's security cooperation with Western powers, plus the severe disruption of economic and humanitarian support as missions shift outside Iraq.

Notes

1 U.S. Department of Defense, Counter–Islamic State of Iraq and Syria (ISIS) Train and Equip Fund (CTEF) Request, FY2021, 22, https://comptroller.defense.gov/Portals/45/Documents/defbudget/fy2021/fy2021_CTEF_J-Book.pdf; and CTEF Request, FY2022, 9, https://comptroller.defense.gov/Portals/45/Documents/defbudget/FY2022/FY2022_CTEF_J-Book.pdf.
2 CTEF Request, FY2021, p. 22, and CTEF Request, FY2022, p. 9.
3 Ibid.
4 U.S. Department of Defense Office of Inspector General, "Lead Inspector General for Operation Inherent Resolve Quarterly Report to the U.S. Congress, January 1–March 31, 2021," 39.
5 U.S. Department of Defense Office of Inspector General, "Lead Inspector General for Operation Inherent Resolve Quarterly Report to the U.S. Congress, April 1–June 30, 2021," 30 in the twelve-month snapshot of June 2020 to May 2021.
6 U.S. Department of Defense, "Joint Publication 3-22: Foreign Internal Defense," August 17, 2018, and February 2, 2021, ix, available at https://www.jcs.mil/Portals/36/Documents/Doctrine/pubs/jp3_22.pdf?ver=2018-10-10-112450-103.
7 Ibid.
8 These deaths can be compared to twenty-four U.S. military deaths in the same period in Afghanistan. See U.S. Department of Defense, "Casualty Status as of 10 a.m. EDT September 20, 2021," https://www.defense.gov/casualty.pdf.
9 U.S. State Department Fact Sheet, "U.S. Security Cooperation with Jordan," Bureau of Political-Military Affairs, May 21, 2021, https://www.state.gov/u-s-security-cooperation-with-jordan/.
10 Jumana Kawar, "Jordan: U.S. Security Assistance and Border Defense Capacity Building," Middle East Institute, October 6, 2020, https://www.mei.edu/publications/jordan-us-security-assistance-and-border-defense-capacity-building.
11 U.S. State Department Fact Sheet, "U.S. Security Cooperation with Jordan," https://www.state.gov/u-s-security-cooperation-with-jordan/.
12 The United States has $4.47 billion in active government-to-government sales cases with Jordan under the Foreign Military Sales (FMS)

system. Since 2016, the United States has also authorized the permanent export of more than $697 million in defense articles to Jordan via the Direct Commercial Sales process. U.S. State Department Fact Sheet, "U.S. Security Cooperation with Jordan," https://www.state.gov/u-s-security-cooperation-with-jordan/.

13 The United States has supported the Jordan Border Security Program, an integrated surveillance, detection, and interdiction system along 350 miles of Jordan's land borders, since the program started in 2009, at a cost of more than $234 million. U.S. State Department Fact Sheet, "U.S. Security Cooperation with Jordan," https://www.state.gov/u-s-security-cooperation-with-jordan/.

14 "Washington Army National Guard Completes Jordan Rotation, Transfers Mission to the Illinois Guard," American Military News, June 16, 2020, https://americanmilitarynews.com/ai/washington-army-national-guard-completes-jordan-rotation-transfers-mission-to-the-illinois-guard/.

15 Barbara Opall-Rome, "Raytheon-Jordan Border Defense Against ISIS Enters Final Phase," Defense News, May 26, 2016, https://www.defensenews.com/global/mideast-africa/2016/05/26/raytheon-jordan-border-defense-against-isis-enters-final-phase/.

16 Mick Mulroy and Eric Oehlerich, "A Tale of Two Partners: Comparing Two Approaches for Partner Force Operations," Middle East Institute, January 29, 2020, https://www.mei.edu/publications/tale-two-partners-comparing-two-approaches-partner-force-operations.

17 For insights into how to better structure U.S. security cooperation to reflect Middle East social and military culture, see Michael J. Eisenstadt and Kenneth M. Pollack, "Training Better Arab Armies," *Parameters* 50, no. 3 (2020), https://press.armywarcollege.edu/parameters/vol50/iss3/10.

1

The ISF Today: House of Cards, or "Good Enough"?

In summer 2014, less than three years after the end of the $26 billion U.S. security assistance effort, a sizable portion of the Iraqi security forces (ISF) disintegrated due to a mixture of battlefield defeats, abandonment by its leaders, and infectious panic.[1] Six divisions (five army and one Federal Police) collapsed to the extent that they never rebuilt.[2] The "will to fight" of the Iraqi military was openly doubted by U.S. military officers in the same way that President Joe Biden suggested the Afghan National Security Forces (ANSF) were "not willing to fight."[3] Almost a third of Iraq was occupied by the Islamic State, and it took nearly forty months before the last areas of IS territorial control in Iraq were liberated in 2017.

Fast-forward to the present day, and the ISF is looking considerably better. As the following text will detail, the Islamic State is not able to control populated places during daylight hours, its activities inside Iraq's cities are extremely subdued, and it has almost ceased mounting external operations against the U.S. homeland and persons. IS operates in tiny cells, usually only mounting tactical operations to secure its immediate surroundings and extort sustenance from local communities. Iraq's most pressing security challenge is increasingly the Iran-backed militias that feed off the state security budget and are enmeshed in the ISF in many locations, complicating the further degradation of IS in its rural hiding sites. The ISF—not the U.S.-led coalition—now provides the vast majority of the resources and *all* the ground combat forces in the counter-IS campaign. This relative self-reliance—versus the situation in Afghanistan, or indeed the negative impact on ISF when the United States withdrew in 2011—is a deliberate result of the post-2014 U.S. engagement in Iraq, which has stressed Iraq as leading and the coalition as supporting. As one U.S. security cooperation manager noted:

> Up to 2011, our mentality was: "We'll fight the enemy, and drag ISF along with us and give them the credit whenever we can." After 2014, our view changed to, "You do it, we will stand right behind you," and we made them fight it their way with their own forces.[4]

The wisdom of that approach is now bearing fruit. The ISF is not a force fighting for survival against a powerfully growing enemy, as was the case with the ANSF and Taliban, but rather a military that has *already* succeeded in its basic mission of containing IS. The trick now is to cement the gains so that backsliding does not require again starting from scratch in the aftermath of some new collapse.

Leadership: Foundation of Success, Sound Basis for Hope

In the first half of 2014, under Prime Minister Nouri al-Maliki, the leadership of the ISF had reached a nadir of professionalism. As the United States undertook a phased military withdrawal from Iraq in 2009–11, Maliki stripped capable officers out of senior commands and replaced them with politically reliable cronies, whose unprofessionalism showed itself in corruption, sectarianism, and ineptitude and cowardice in battle. In 2012–14, the ISF—which had reached a good level of U.S.-enabled capability in 2009 but which needed constant U.S. support—quickly rotted from the head downward. In combination with an aggressive and growing adversary, the Islamic State of 2012–14, the result was extreme frailty within ISF formations. It took only a single battlefield defeat in Mosul to shatter a large fraction of the entire force.

Since 2014, the professionalization of the ISF command cadre has consistently mirrored the quality of leadership demonstrated in the Iraqi Prime Minister's Office. Prime Minister Haider al-Abadi achieved huge steps forward following the June 2014 collapse of the Iraqi military, performing a major command reshuffle that saved the ISF and justified U.S.-led security assistance to Iraq. Then Iraq backslid to an alarming degree in 2018–20 under the short-lived government of Prime Minister Adil Abdulmahdi, with Iran-backed militias gaining prominence over the professional officer cadre.

Since 2020, Iraq has moved in the right direction again, with Prime Minister Mustafa al-Kadhimi undertaking a rolling series of command reshuffles that have brought younger, more capable officers to the fore. As figure 1.1 shows, the pace of command changes has been steady and the results positive. Today, most of the ISF—i.e., all elements except the Popular Mobilization Forces (PMF)—are centrally commanded from the Joint Operations Center–Iraq (JOC-I), which videoconferences and otherwise communicates with provincial or multi-province Operations Commands (OCs). There is a rudimentary JOC-I campaign plan for the phasing of activities and operations each year,[5] and it guides ISF actions in an appropriately broad manner. Iraq initiates security operations at the JOC-I level (coordinating multiple OCs in multi-division operations), at the OC level (usually divisional or below), and at the local level (battalion or single-brigade operations, initiated at local initiative). Six liaison headquarters have been established between the JOC-I and Kurdistan Region of Iraq (KRI) security forces. Continuous ISF operations against IS have been used to refine local command arrangements and weed out weak commanders from battlefield service in the so-called hot areas where the jihadist group is still active.

Figure 1.1. ISF Command Table

Command	Name of Commander	Quality of Commander ☐ Very low risk ▨ Low risk ■ High risk	Improvement (+), Same (=), or Deterioration (–) in Quality
Prime Minister–National Operations Center (PM-NOC)	Thiya al-Musawi	☐	=
Deputy Chief of Staff–Operations (DCOS-Ops)	Staff LTG Abdul-Amir Yarallah	☐	=
Deputy Chief of Staff–Training (DCOS-Training)	LTG Hamid Muhammad Kamar replaced LTG Salahuddin Mustafa (Mar 2021)	☐	+
Deputy Chief of Staff–Logistics (DCOS-Logistics)	LTG Ali Muhammad Salim al-Araji	▨	=
Deputy Chief of Staff–Administration (DCOS-Admin)	MG Muhammad al-Bayati replaced LTG Abdul-Amir al-Zaidi (Sep 2021)	▨	+
Iraqi Air Force	LTG Shihab Jahid Ali	▨	=
Iraqi Army Aviation	MG Samir Zaki	☐	=
Iraqi Air Defense Command	MG Maan al-Saadi replaced MG Jabbar Obeid (May 2020)	☐	+
Federal Police Command	MG Saleh Nasr al-Ameri replaced LTG Jaafar al-Battat (Jan 2021)	▨	=
Counter-Terrorism Service (CTS)	GEN Abdul-Wahab al-Saadi replaced GEN Talib Shaghati al-Kenani (May 2020)	☐	+
Counter Terrorism Command (CTC)	MG Karim al-Tamimi replaced MG Alaa al-Fayyadh (May 2020)	☐	+

Figure 1.1. ISF Command Table (continued)

Command	Name of Commander	Quality of Commander ☐ Very low risk ▨ Low risk ■ High risk	Improvement (+), Same (=), or Deterioration (–) in Quality
International Zone Security Division	MG Hamid al-Zuhairi replaced MG Nasir al-Khikhani (Aug 2020)	☐	+
Baghdad Operations Command (BOC)	MG Ahmed Salim Bahjat al-Utaibi replaced LTG Qais al-Muhammadawi (Jan 2021)	☐	+
Diyala Operations Command (DOC)	MG Raad Mahmoud Bishr replaced MG Ghassan al-Izzi (Sep 2020)	▨	=
Anbar Operations Command (AOC)	MG Nasser Ghanim al-Hiti	▨	=
Jazira and Badia Operations Command (JBOC)	MG Hamid al-Nams al-Jabbouri replaced MG Ahmed Salim Bahjat al-Utaibi (Jan 2021)	▨	=
Samarra Operations Command (SamOC)	MG Jabbar Hatim al-Darraji replaced LTG Imad al-Zuhairi (Sep 2020)	▨	+
	MG Ali Mashgal replaced MG Jabbar Hatim al-Darraji (Mar 2021)	▨	=
Salah al-Din Operations Command (SaDOC)	MG Abdul-Mohsen al-Abbasi	▨	=

Figure 1.1. ISF Command Table (continued)

Command	Name of Commander	Quality of Commander ☐Very low risk ▨Low risk ■High risk	Improvement (+), Same (=), or Deterioration (–) in Quality
Nineveh Operations Command (NiOC)	MG Ismail Shibab al-Mahlawi replaced MG Numan al-Zubaie (Aug 2020)	☐	=
	MG Mahmoud al-Falahi replaced MG Ismail Shibab al-Mahlawi (Mar 2021)	☐	+
Western Nineveh Operations Command (NiOC-West)	MG Jabbar Naima al-Tai	▨	=
Joint Forces Command–Kirkuk (JFC-K)	LTG Ali Jassim al-Furaiji replaced LTG Saad al-Harbiyah (Jun 2021)	■	–
Basra Operations Command (BaOC)	MG Akram Saddam replaced LTG Qassim Nazzal al-Maliki (Aug 2020)	▨	+
	MG Ali al-Majidi replaced MG Akram Saddam (May 2021)	▨	=
Furat al-Awsat Operations Command (FAOC)	MG Ali al-Hashemi	▨	=
Sumer Operations Command (SuOC)	LTG Saad al-Harbiyah replaced MG Imad al-Silawi (Jun 2021)	▨	+

Force Design and Deployment

Iraq's security forces face typical contending pressures—too many tasks and not enough resources—but in a much more urgent and deadly setting than most militaries. Besides capabilities needed to counter threats from other states (e.g., air defense, sea control, and heavy ground forces), the ISF currently needs sufficient forces to accomplish the following internal security missions:

- Rural counterinsurgency and counterterrorism against IS in "hot" areas of the following provinces (Anbar, Babil, Baghdad, Diyala, Kirkuk, Nineveh, and Salah al-Din)

- Counterterrorism intelligence and direct action in all provinces, including major cities, against both IS and uncontrolled armed militias

- Border control along the "hot" border with Syria (605 km), plus other borders with Turkey, Iran, Saudi Arabia, Jordan, and Kuwait[6]

- Internal border policing (on both sides) of the dividing line between federal Iraq's fifteen provinces and the four-province KRI, totaling 590 kilometers

- Urban and rural law enforcement, including maintenance of law and order in remote, well-armed tribal areas in southern Iraq and Kurdistan

Despite this mission set, the economically challenged Iraqi state has begun to downsize its commitment of resources to defense and security spending. For instance, in the 2021 budget, Iraq's Ministry of Defense funds were reduced by 25.6 percent, the Counter Terrorism Service (CTS) lost 19.9 percent of funding, and the Ministry of Interior lost 9.3 percent.[7] Hiring for the security forces has largely been capped, with the exception of a 20,000-billet expansion of the Popular Mobilization Forces (PMF) and a one-month special payment to 30,000 more unregistered PMF fighters in May–September 2021.[8] The Iraqi government has stopped raising new ISF tactical units (brigades), for example, canceling the establishment of a 19th division, Iraqi army, in 2020. The focus is on strengthening existing formations and consolidating higher-than-brigade unit functions into fewer commands in order to reduce the number of headquarters and share enabler units (intelligence, artillery, and logistics). (See figure 1.2.)

Figure 1.2. Iraq Budget Funding for Security Institutions, 2019 and 2021

Security Institution	2019*	2021*	Change
Ministry of Defense	6,370,627,858	4,737,383,176	-25.6%
National Security Council	160,626,702	164,808,224	2.6%
Iraqi National Intelligence Service	177,324,334	186,756,810	5.3%
Ministry of Interior	7,928,501,216	7,188,835,401	-9.3%
Popular Mobilization Commission	1,823,861,830	2,134,107,230	17%
Counter Terrorism Service	519,208,973	415,998,941	-19.9%
Borders Ports Authority	30,960,998	31,159,103	-0.6%
Military Industrialization Corporation	—	5,683,429	—

*Notes: Budget figures are adjusted for inflation so will differ from public government documents; there was no budget in 2020.

Source: U.S. Defense Intelligence Agency, response to Defense Department Office of Inspector General request for information, 21.3 OIR 065, 6/28/2021.

There are remaining inefficiencies in how Iraq uses its security manpower, for example, in the duplication of PMF and non-PMF presence in the same areas of responsibility, which has more to do with militia economic rackets and political actions than with meeting the genuine security needs of Iraq. The most glaring example of PMF military overreach is the militia presence along the Syria-Iraq border, where the composition of the PMF units—the mostly Iran-backed units, consisting largely of southern Shia—is entirely alien to the anti-Iran local Sunni population (see figures 1.3 and 1.4).

Figure 1.3. ISF Personnel

	November 2009		January 2015		August 2021	
	Brigade equiva-lents	On-duty combat strength	Brigade equiva-lents	On-duty combat strength	Brigade equiva-lents	On-duty combat strength
Iraqi army	55	210,000	40	48,000 (60%)	58	58,000 (50%)
Federal Police	30	120,000	24	36,000 (75%)	27	20,500 (50%)
CTS	3	10,500	3	10,000 (100%)	3	8,000 (70%)
PMF			20	30,000 (25%)	30	45,000 (33%)
Kurdistan Region security forces	47	80,000	54	81,000 (75%)	54	56,000 (50%)
TOTAL	135	420,500	141	237,000	172	187,500

Note: In 2009, at the apex of ISF manpower, units were regularly maintained at above-establishment strength to allow for maximum manning even when leave and attrition were factored in. By 2015, units were engaged in major combat operations, but still displayed varying levels of actual manning. PMF units never achieved a high frontline manning level, with personnel largely operating in a part-time mode, or effectively operating as a paid reserve that only periodically reported for duty. In addition, the PMF maintained the highest proportion of billets (within the ISF) filled by "ghost soldiers," who existed only on paper to allow their units to fraudulently claim a paycheck. After the end of major combat operations, many ISF units temporarily reduced their on-duty manning levels to lower their operating costs, while the PMF increased theirs slightly, reflecting improvements in their operating budget.

Figure 1.4. Order of Battle Map

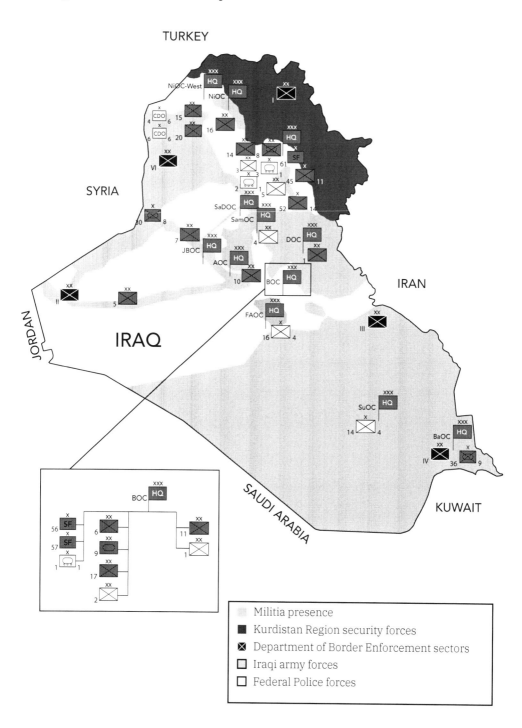

Rationalization and Redeployment

Facing expectations of reduced funds and (hopefully) a reduced mission set, the ISF has envisioned a gradual rationalization of its deployment, roles, and missions since major counter-IS combat operations ended with the liberation of all cities in 2017. The army is increasingly focused on a "rural and border" role in the future, and the Federal Police may revert to a motorized urban public order force. Department of Border Enforcement brigades have been strengthened along the "hot" border with Syria and reinforced with twinned Iraqi army brigades in some areas and overlapped with PMF units in other areas. The process of shuffling army units out of urban settings and into rural "hot" areas and other rural settings has begun, while Federal Police brigades are slowly being shifted to urban settings and the rural "belts" of cities such as Samarra and Baghdad. The redeployment of entire ISF divisions to new areas on the basis of their suitability for the destination is a comparatively novel and welcome phenomenon. Iraq has even used its large multi-division counterinsurgency operations to specifically identify weak units that might be rotated out of "hot" areas and stronger units that can backfill them—for instance, in Tarmiyah and northern Diyala province, where more capable ISF units have been brought in to supplant or overlap militias and weak ISF units.

Another incomplete aspect of optimizing the deployment of the ISF is the closing of gaps between federal and KRI forces along the internal federal-KRI border (the 590 km Kurdistan Control Line, or KCL). These gaps are not uniform along the KCL: the map (see figure 1.5) shows the variety of diagnosed challenges along the breadth of the KCL. Effective control of difficult terrain is the key, including establishment of clearer lines of control, increased ISF force density south of the KCL, and joint patrolling near the KCL by better-integrated federal-KRI security structures. The over-garrisoning of the relatively safe Kurdistan Region and the inability to deploy any of its forces south of the KCL is a major inefficiency that costs Iraq dearly. The establishment of six federal-KRI Joint Coordination Centers (Baghdad, Erbil, Diyala, Kirkuk, Makhmur, and Nineveh)[9] is an important step forward in solving this issue, albeit a necessary rather than sufficient one. The first

Figure 1.5. Kurdistan Control Line Map

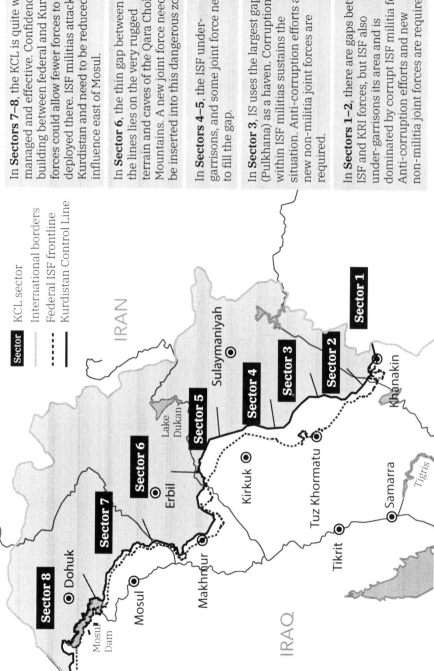

new amalgamated federal-KRI units, capable of working both sides of the KCL, are being formed in Sectors 1–3 (Khanaqin to Tuz Khormatu). As later sections will explore, the U.S.-led international community can do much more to encourage efficiencies along the KCL.

Counterterrorism Operations

Unlike their Afghan equivalents, the ISF faces a greatly diminished threat from its main historic foe, the Islamic State. As noted earlier, IS remains entrenched across northern and central Iraq but is limited to a weak, low-level rural insurgency. As regular clearance operations into the Islamic State's rural sanctuaries show, the group is unable to deny terrain to government forces even in its core areas. In terms of overall activity, the insurgency has stabilized roughly at the level it achieved in 2012, shortly after the U.S. withdrawal. The insurgency is particularly weak in urban centers, where IS terrorist networks have been almost entirely uprooted since 2017. The Islamic State's ability to conduct coordinated, mass-casualty attacks has also been heavily degraded. This state of affairs marks a major contrast to the insurgency's previous low point in 2010–11, when car bombings and other urban attacks were still a semi-regular occurrence. The group's leadership has been more or less continuously decimated since 2015 and remains under intense pressure inside Iraq. Finally, although Islamic State networks in countries bordering Iraq are still important to the group's functioning, there are few signs these cells are capable of mounting external attack operations against the U.S. homeland or even other regional states.[10]

Today's ISF has the tough job of further whittling down the remaining elements of the IS insurgency. Borders must be secured so that IS cannot recover capability by bringing veterans and newly adolescent IS fighters from al-Hawl camp in Syria[11] and from Turkey, both havens where the IS cadres sheltered after the territorial defeat of the Caliphate. New IS recruiting must not benefit from the long-term garrisoning of Sunni "liberated" areas by primarily Shia militias from other parts of Iraq. The elimination of the jihadist group's residual cells will be a slow process that relies upon the full spectrum of development and resettlement of civilians, not just upon security operations. Aside from static security operations (checkpoints, observation posts, and patrols), the two main military mechanisms in use at the present time are (1) conventional military (i.e., army, Federal Police, and PMF) rural "clearance" operations, and (2) intelligence-based counterterrorism raids. In the authors' views, the latter targeted activities are becoming increasingly important as the size of IS cells diminishes and their mode of operating grows more covert. Sustainment and human resource management are essential for resetting today's burned-out ISF units and equipment from the sprint of 2014–17 to the marathon of finishing off IS and emergent militia challenges.

Clearance Operations

The U.S. Congress's quarterly Inspector General reports on Operation Inherent Resolve give a clear picture of the corps-, division-, and battalion-level clearance operations still taking place in the "hot" provinces like Kirkuk, Diyala, Nineveh, Anbar, and southern Salah al-Din. Such operations have a pro forma feel, akin to "mowing the grass." In each brigade area, commanders feel an ongoing expectation to mount a number of operations each month in response to local reporting of IS activities and "bed down" locations—e.g., some part of a wadi (streambed, often dry) system or an abandoned hamlet. Occasionally, multiple brigades or even multiple divisions and OCs will take part, as was the case with the Heroes of Iraq series of major clearance operations in 2020.

Each operation is a slow-moving, daylight, ground-based clearance effort, with IS gaining significant advance notice of ISF intentions because of the difficulty of quickly approaching their rural redoubts over rough terrain. IS personnel tend to escape but usually some of their "bed down" sites and arms caches are found and destroyed, and dense vegetation is defoliated by burning and bulldozing. Rather than being viewed by ISF commanders as decisive operations, these clearing operations keep the ISF units active, show some support to beleaguered local rural communities, and pressure

IS cells to constantly move and reduce the pace of operations so that they may recover from attrition. Clearance operations are thus necessary but not sufficient to secure the long-term suppression of IS.

The clearance operations unveil certain ongoing weaknesses in the ISF. The overstretched ISF only sweeps through rural terrain, rarely establishing a permanent presence there, because it is undermanned and lacks the field engineering and nighttime quick-reaction forces to build and support outposts that can protect it at night. Therefore, local villagers are usually exposed at night and are too fearful to inform on IS cells. The ISF has a proven capacity to sustain the tempo of such clearance operations without significant external inputs but only at a cost of cannibalizing spare parts and by replacing armored vehicles with unarmored pickup trucks. Because of the predictable nature of the clearance operations and the use of unarmored vehicles, IS ambushes and booby traps are often effective in killing and injuring small numbers of ISF troops during each major operation. The morale of ISF soldiers is weakened by the lack of combat lifesaving and medical evacuation capacity.

In a sign of progress, Iraq's Army Aviation Command (which controls armed helicopters) is increasing the number of Air Weapons Teams it embeds with troops on clearance operations, allowing more operations to benefit from aerial observation and fire support. Nevertheless, daylight operations are often ineffective in trapping IS personnel because the ISF lacks density in its aerial surveillance capabilities (due to limited drone and aircraft serviceability and endurance) and also lacks sufficient precision time-sensitive target engagement options (helicopter-borne commandos, armed drones and aircraft, and precision artillery). As a result, IS remains hard to track and hard to reach in bad terrain.

Targeted Counterterrorism Raids

The other, higher-impact activities of the counter-IS campaign are nocturnal and daytime raids by special forces, often in collaboration with the U.S.-led coalition's intelligence and aerial forces. At the more advanced end of the spectrum, the Counter Terrorism Service and equivalent Kurdish forces (Counter-Terrorism Department and Counter-Terrorism Group) work with the U.S.-led coalition and Kurdish intelligence agencies to raid and strike high-value IS targets. CTS and its Ministry of Interior counterpart, the Emergency Response Division, also work with the more effective Iraqi intelligence services (Iraqi National Intelligence Service, Ministry of Interior Federal Information and Investigations Agency, and National Security Service, or NSS) to undertake mid-value targeting. At the local level, the NSS and military intelligence agencies work with local ground-holding army and police units to mount raids against lower-level targets. The majority of confirmed IS detentions and deaths are caused by these warrant-based, targeted operations. The Iraq Train and Equip Fund, a U.S. project, has undoubtedly succeeded in creating effective counterterrorism raiding forces, in particular the CTS, which routinely raises the effectiveness of all Iraqi forces that it partners with. Yet the CTS is overused for this precise reason, and yet also underfunded, resulting in an aging and exhausted manpower pool and too few new recruits. As a result, CTS capabilities are slowly backsliding because of overuse and under-resourcing.

Level of Iraqi Reliance on U.S.-Led Forces

In the narrow case of CTS, U.S. support is still undoubtedly pivotal in maintaining the service's unique level of professionalism and capability, albeit in low-visibility ways and at little cost. (The CTS has been allocated $4.78 million in the fiscal year 2022 budgetary request for the Counter–Islamic State Train and Equip Fund, or CTEF).[12] Compared to the broader ISF, the coalition's Special Operations Advisor Group gives the compact CTS an unparalleled level of support that includes training, administrative and financial procurement support, and dedicated intelligence and aerial support.

The U.S.-led coalition also provides specialized training[13] and collocated "advise, assist, and enable" support to the senior commanders and small groups within the JOC-I in Baghdad and its northern equivalent at Erbil. Akin to "management consultancy," the U.S. advisors react to requests from Iraqi leaders and focus their efforts on helping JOC-I think about intelligence, planning, aviation, and fire support. As a result of collocation, the U.S. advisors at JOC-I engage with the Iraqi leadership via nightly conversations and a detailed weekly operations and intelligence brief.[14] A final area of unique and heavy reliance is the Kurdistan Region's receipt of $240 million per year of stipends to its Peshmerga forces, which will be discussed later. The stipends are a lever to encourage Peshmerga reforms sought by America and have been effective in overcoming party-political barriers to the nonpartisan reintegration of Peshmerga heavy weapons units and a number of unified Regional Guard Brigades.

Minimal U.S. Role in Training, Equipping, and Sustaining Ground Forces

Elsewhere, the picture is very different, underlining the reality that *the United States is uninvolved in most aspects of ISF training, sustainment, and operations.* For instance, the U.S. military no longer trains any Iraqi tactical units, aside from small programs with CTS and other special forces. The Covid-19 pandemic ended large-scale training even before the coalition announced an end to its unit training activities in 2020. The train and equip funding in the requested CTEF for Iraq dropped from $282.8 million in FY2021 to $20 million requested in FY2022.[15] The coalition's train-the-trainer activities in 2018–20 conveniently unfolded shortly before Iraq was forced to rely upon its own training resources. Iraq training today is very uneven in quality: only praetorian units like the armored forces of the 9th division of the Iraqi army and special forces regularly train at hubs like Academia in Area IV in Baghdad or Taji Centralized Training Facility. Most units remain on a frontline almost without relief: if they are taken off a "hot area," it is to be rested in a quiet area rather than sent through refresher training. The ISF will probably not engage in regular training cycles until units are regularly rotated off the frontline and an identified set of threats—IS and rogue militias—are codified into training syllabi.

Nor does the U.S. government directly maintain any ISF equipment fleets now, with fleet-wide maintenance of Iraqi ground vehicles by the U.S. military largely a thing of the past. In the FY2022 requested CTEF package for Iraq, the previous year's $24 million budget for spare parts was entirely removed.[16] Sustainment support dropped from $124.2 million in FY2021 to $20 million in the FY2022 request.[17] With the exception of the Kurdistan Region, Iraq now largely maintains its own vehicle fleets. As the second-quarter 2021 Inspector General report to Congress notes: "the Iraqis resolve logistics and sustainment issues internally, with no further discussion with the coalition."[18] The bald truth is, considering the security and payment risks of working in federal Iraq, many U.S. companies are not currently interested in long-term maintenance contracts, even if they were sufficiently funded and approved smoothly by Iraq.

Even so, Iraq's sustainment situation appears to be neither ideal nor urgently bad. The lower tempo of operations across the ISF (when compared to the era of major combat operations) has reduced strain on vehicle fleets. Iraqi military mechanics are highly skilled in the "good enough" upkeep of Hummers and other military trucks, which are the backbone of the ISF. Salvage and cannibalization are powerful tools because of the extraordinary number of U.S.-provided vehicles in Iraq after two decades of operations. There is also a large and effective, if expensive, "gray market" for knock-off imported copies of U.S. spare parts. Likewise, there are some effective, if rough-and-ready, depot maintenance systems, for instance, the Federal Police's system for keeping armored security vehicles on the road. Iraq *can* keep enough vehicles in operation to sustain clearances and general ISF operations, though there is clearly room for improvement.

Adequate Sustainment of ISF Air Operations

Sustainment of air forces is more challenging but still manageable. At the most demanding end, Lockheed Martin support to the F-16 program has been disrupted by periodic removal of its twenty-five contractors from the endangered Balad base (where they were threatened by Iran-backed militias) to Erbil.[19] Nevertheless, with local capacity and creative workarounds by contractors,[20] the F-16 kept flying throughout this disruption, contrary to some reporting. In the second quarter of 2021, F-16s flew 360 training missions and 13 strike missions.[21] The limiting factor on F-16 strike operations was not aircraft mission availability, which was 82 percent for strike operations. Rather, it was too few strike opportunities overall, and even fewer that required Iraqi F-16s rather than the capabilities of Iraqi helicopters or other platforms.[22]

Other key U.S.-supported intelligence, surveillance, and reconnaissance (ISR) platforms (King Air 350 and AC/RC-208 Armed Caravan) also had acceptable (82%) mission availability.[23] Although awaiting a software patch, the U.S.-supported Scan Eagle drone fleet had a 90 percent mission availability for line-of-sight operations (i.e., they are mechanically flight-ready).[24] In comparison, supposedly hardy Russian-built systems like Mi-28, Su-25, and Mi-35 have mission availability rates of 6–20 percent because of a lack of spare parts, while none of Iraq's twenty Chinese CH-4 armed drones are operational at the time of writing.[25] Although short of funds and spare parts, Iraq's transport helicopter fleet (including many Russian-built helicopters supported by U.S.-sourced spare parts) still achieves mission availability rates of 65–80 percent and now provides the aerial lift for most CTS raids.[26] The United States also does not refuel Iraqi aircraft over Iraq because Iraq has not chosen to join the U.S. Air Tasking Order yet, which is a necessary step before aerial refueling is an option.

Direct Non-Combat Support and Remaining "Combat Operations"

Finally, the U.S. military in Iraq is no longer providing much lethal air cover to Iraqi units on the ground. U.S. ISR aircraft and drones *do* provide vital intelligence support, especially because of their superior sensors and endurance by virtue of not requiring frequent refueling. Online transponder tracking services show multiple nightly passes by U.S. ISR assets over "hot" areas such as Kirkuk, northern Diyala, and Anbar. A survey of one month of tracks for U.S. ISR aircraft shows the United States flies four ISR platforms over Iraq on an average night (mainly King Air 350s, MQ-9 Reapers, and MQ-1C Gray Eagles). Additionally, the United States maintains a combat air patrol (CAP) over coalition bases at night, involving F-15E or F-16 aircraft, or both, plus the requisite refueling tanker support. These CAP missions have little to do with IS but instead are used to deter or detect Iran-backed militias striking coalition sites.

Yet the number of strikes each month by U.S. and coalition aircraft remains low. As figure 1.6 notes, coalition strikes in Iraq averaged 7.2 per month in the twelve-month snapshot of June 2020 to May 2021. Of these, most were used to safely demolish IS caves and blow up IS ammunition caches in place. Thus, part of the remaining minor U.S. combat role in Iraq is a "nice to have" effort to save ISF a dangerous job but hardly a mission-critical capability that ISF should rely upon. In 2022, such coalition strikes will probably cease, and the United States must carefully watch the effect on IS activity. If the United States senses that the pressure on IS leadership is critically declining and that IS cells are showing step changes in capability, it should be ready to answer any reasonable request for direct kinetic support, possibly under the request for more authorization from Congress or under Title 50, involving single strikes or short campaigns against leadership networks. Naturally, the president also retains the right, under Article 2 of the U.S. Constitution, to direct military action to protect and defend U.S. forces in Iraq.

Figure 1.6 CJTF-OIR Strike Summary Report

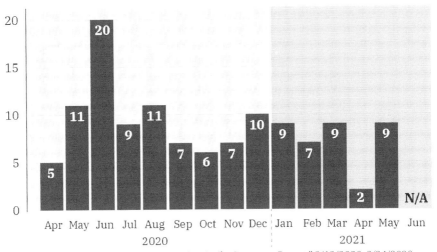

Sources: CJTF-OIR, press releases, "CJTF-OIR Strike Summary Report," 2/13/2020, 3/24/2020, 4/30/2020, 6/24/2020, 9/8/2020, 10/29/2020, 12/14/2020, 1/6/2021, 2/4/2021, 7/6/2021, and 7/7/2021.

Notes

1 Alex Park, "$26 Billion in U.S. Aid Later, the Iraqi Military Is a Total Disaster," *Mother Jones*, September 25, 2014, available at https://www.motherjones.com/politics/2014/09/iraq-army-security-force-billions/.

2 Michael Knights, *The Long Haul: Rebooting U.S. Security Cooperation in Iraq*, Policy Focus 137 (Washington DC: Washington Institute, 2015), https://www.washingtoninstitute.org/policy-analysis/long-haul-rebooting-us-security-cooperation-iraq.

3 Rachel Pannett et al., "Biden Defends Decision to Withdraw from Afghanistan After Taliban's Rapid Return to Power," *Washington Post*, August 6, 2021, https://www.washingtonpost.com/world/2021/08/16/afghanistan-kabul-taliban-live-updates/.

4 Author interview, single U.S. contact, 2021 (exact date, name, and places withheld at request of the interviewee).

5 U.S. Department of Defense, "Lead Inspector General for Operation Inherent Resolve Quarterly Report to the U.S. Congress, January 1–March 31, 2021," 32.

6 Iraq has land borders with Turkey (352 km), Iran (1,458 km), Kuwait (240 km), Saudi Arabia (814 km), Jordan (181 km), and Syria (605 km)—3,650 kilometers in total. Lt. Col. Steven Oluic, "Iraq's Border Security," *CTC Sentinel* 2, no. 1 (2009), https://ctc.usma.edu/iraqs-border-security-key-to-an-iraqi-endstate/.

7 U.S. Department of Defense, "Lead Inspector General for Operation Inherent Resolve Quarterly Report to the U.S. Congress, April 1–June 30, 2021," April 1–June 30, 2021," 43.

8 Sura Ali, "PM Kadhimi Promises to Return 30,000 Former PMF fighters to Service," Rudaw, December 5, 2021, https://www.rudaw.net/english/middleeast/iraq/120520213.

9 "Operation Inherent Resolve Quarterly Report, April 1–June 30, 2021," 35.

10 See Michael Knights and Alex Almeida, "Remaining and Expanding: The Recovery of Islamic State Operations in Iraq in 2019–2020," *CTC Sentinel* 13, no. 5 (2020), https://ctc.usma.edu/remaining-and-expanding-the-recovery-of-islamic-state-operations-in-iraq-in-2019-2020/. Also see "Can the Islamic State Make a Comeback in Iraq Part 3? Interview with Horizon's Alex Mello," *Musings on Iraq*, August 19, 2019,

http://musingsoniraq.blogspot.com/2019/08/can-islamic-state-make-comeback-in-iraq.html.

11 As Iraq's national security advisor, Qasim al-Araji, told a conference on August 31, 2021: "Al-Hawl camp, located in Syria thirteen kilometers away from the Iraqi border, contains more than 70,000 people, 30,760 of whom are Iraqi citizens. Thirty thousand are Syrian citizens, and the remaining 10,000 are foreigners, including foreign fighters. Five hundred Iraqi families have requested to come back to Iraq. The situation in al-Hawl has to be taken seriously. We have reached out to the international community, coalition forces, and ambassadors to Iraq on this matter and asked for their support in order to find a solution. The situation is quite concerning at al-Hawl, taking the bad environment into consideration. More than 20,000 of the 30,760 Iraqis in al-Hawl are under eighteen years old or female. NSA assesses that al-Hawl camp poses a huge threat to national security. Therefore, the problem has to be taken seriously and handled." The video of the conference can be found on the following link: www.youtube.com/watch?v=D9AEwcaMKuc.

12 U.S. Department of Defense, Counter–Islamic State Train of Iraq and Syria and Equip Fund (CTEF) Request, FY2022, 7–9, https://comptroller.defense.gov/Portals/45/Documents/defbudget/FY2022/FY2022_CTEF_J-Book.pdf.

13 In the first quarter of 2021, the coalition undertook sixteen seminars on targeting, civil affairs, intelligence collection planning, information operations, and artillery operations. U.S. Department of Defense, "Lead Inspector General for Operation Inherent Resolve Quarterly Report to the U.S. Congress, January 1–March 31, 2021," 31.

14 U.S. Department of Defense, "Operation Inherent Resolve Quarterly Report, April 1–June 30, 2021," 33.

15 U.S. Department of Defense, Counter–Islamic State Train and Equip Fund (CTEF) Request, FY2021, 22, https://comptroller.defense.gov/Portals/45/Documents/defbudget/fy2021/fy2021_CTEF_J-Book.pdf; Counter–Islamic State Train and Equip Fund Request, FY2022, 9, https://comptroller.defense.gov/Portals/45/Documents/defbudget/FY2022/FY2022_CTEF_J-Book.pdf.

16 CTEF Request, FY2021, p. 22, and CTEF Request, FY2022, 9.

17 Ibid.

18 "Operation Inherent Resolve Quarterly Report, April 1–June 30, 2021," 33.

19 Cathy Otten, "Iraq's Failing F-16 Program Highlights Corruption at Balad Airbase," Iraq Oil Report, August 12, 2020, https://www.iraqoilreport.com/news/iraqs-failing-f-16-program-highlights-corruption-at-balad-airbase-42995/.

20 F-16s have been serviced using a number of innovative workarounds: by video-teleconference with Iraqi technicians at Balad, with same-day in-and-out "fly-to-advise" from Erbil, and by taking the F-16s to the technicians at Balad when Iraqi personnel could not provide services. Author interviews, multiple U.S. contacts, 2021 (exact date, name, and places withheld at request of the interviewee).

21 "Operation Inherent Resolve Quarterly Report, April 1–June 30, 2021," 39–40.

22 Ibid., 39.

23 Ibid.

24 Ibid.

25 Ibid.

26 Ibid.

2

The ISF Tomorrow: Where Does It Need to Be?

The previous chapter painted a picture of today's Iraqi security forces. Although very untidy by Western military standards, the ISF today is relatively well led—when Iraq has a capable prime minister—relatively effective, and largely independent, and it does not face anything like the recent Afghanistan scenario. The ISF does not lean heavily on the U.S.-led coalition, and U.S. touch points with the ISF are limited to the very top (the operational brain at JOC-I) and the sharp end (the special forces, intelligence, and air assets that are Iraq's deadliest capabilities). This is a good starting point for this study to transition to the future of the ISF and U.S.-Iraq security cooperation.

The post-caliphate future of the ISF and associated international military support have been on coalition planners' minds for many years. In 2018, the coalition developed a future operating model called Reliable Partnership that envisaged what type of coalition support would be required to "help Iraq be sovereign, stable, and independent, to the degree that it can counter extremism in all forms."[1] The concept remains sound: U.S.-led security cooperation would prioritize the ISF capabilities focused on internal stability, not external defense (i.e., conventional combat against a state-level adversary). Iraq is still many years away from independently deterring Turkish or Iranian aggression within its borders and will have to rely on diplomatic support to minimize these risks. In the near term, Iraq needs security forces that are "good enough" to overcome domestic violent extremists.

Job One: No Backsliding

Iraq is not Afghanistan, and the Islamic State is not the Taliban. At present, Iraq can experience painful strikes from IS but not a grievous blow such as the one the group inflicted in Mosul in June 2014. Even powerful militias nested within the Popular Mobilization Forces and Ministry of Interior can only mobilize a portion of the combat strength available to the Iraqi army, CTS, pro-government PMF, and other loyalist forces (see Annex B). Beyond the raw military balance, the social, political, and religious costs of trying to overthrow the state by coup make such an effort risky for rogue militia groups.

Even so, the ISF is not "complete," because of the proven risk that progress can erode catastrophically over a short period of years. As a detailed Washington Institute study illustrated,[2] when the United States stood behind Iraq, the ISF effectively mastered the counterinsurgency in Mosul, taking Islamic State attacks from a high point of 666 per month in the first quarter of 2008 to an average of 32 attacks in the first quarter of 2011. Then, in 2011–14, as the United States withdrew and ISF leadership deteriorated, the trend reversed until monthly attacks had risen to an average of 297 in the first quarter of 2014.

Long-term ISF watchers know that the problem is not that the ISF has failed to become "good enough" to keep IS at a low level, but rather that it may quickly *cease* to be "good enough" if U.S. assistance is abruptly removed or the military leadership once again is politicized. This is because of a deep-seated fragility and lack of self-confidence in the post-2014 ISF, for which the defeat at Mosul is still fresh. ISF victories were largely won alongside the U.S.-led coalition, and their defeats occurred when the coalition was absent. The potential for backsliding must be especially vivid in the aftermath of the collapse of the Afghan National Security Forces in Kabul, coincident with the withdrawal of U.S. forces. The minimum U.S. objective for the ISF should be no backsliding, either via the politicization of military leadership or the stripping of military budgets to favor militias. Progress in ISF development must be allowed to "set," in the same manner that concrete is left to harden before any supports are removed.

Domestic Primacy, Not Monopoly of Force

A pragmatic U.S. vision of security cooperation with Iraq recognizes that the ISF is hardly an ideal partner—but it is a "good enough" partner. For every CTS or Iraqi army unit, there is a militia-influenced Ministry of Interior or PMF counterpart (see Annex B). This is the reality of working "by, with, and through" partner forces. As figure 2.1 indicates, the level of Iran-backed militia penetration across the ISF varies greatly but is present in all types of units to varying degrees. The difference between the ISF case and that of Lebanon (Hezbollah influence over the Lebanese Armed Forces) is one of degree but a significant difference nonetheless. Hezbollah is the first among equals: in Iraq, the balance of forces is much closer and arguably weighted in the state's favor. For instance, Annex B shows the authors' calculations, which suggest 84,975 loyalist troops on duty on a given day, versus 60,584 Iran-influenced forces. While marbled with militia penetration, the bulk of the ISF is still under the control of the Iraqi government and the situation is tenable and improving, not merely salvageable or declining.

Figure 2.1 Risk Posed by Iran-Backed Militias to ISF

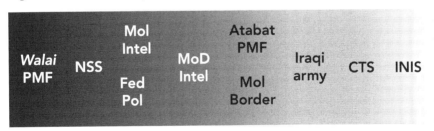

CTS   Counter Terrorism Service
INIS   Iraqi National Intelligence Service
NSS   National Security Service

The graphic above gives the authors' assessment of the level of risk of Iran-backed militia penetration of different ISF organizations. Black indicates the highest level of risk and light gray the lowest. The most penetrated are the "walai" PMF, the Iran-backed militias that believe in Iranian-style religious jurisprudence, velayat-e faqih—hence walai, the Iraqi way to describe such a believer.

Building Loyalist Forces Within Iraq

For some years to come, however, Washington must be clear-sighted that not all ISF members will or can work with the U.S.-led coalition, and some will continue to represent an acute security and counterintelligence threat. Like Afghanistan, Iraq is an environment where advanced U.S. equipment must be subjected to the military's End-Use Monitoring program, and where only elite forces are entrusted with sensitive technologies that they have a good track record of protecting, even at the height of militia penetration.[3] Less sensitive U.S. materiel (guns, trucks, and so on) will sometimes be diverted into militia hands, and a degree of leakage to U.S.-designated Foreign Terrorist Organizations is sadly inevitable in such a chaotic environment. The question for U.S. policymakers is whether the diversion of some American military aid is a worthwhile price for the maintenance of influence over the majority of the ISF. Put another way, is denying pro-Iranian groups access to basic weapons—or indeed to sanctioned Russian weapons purchases— worth deliberately creating a vacuum in Iraq that Iran and Russia will fill to dominate Iraq's future?

U.S. security cooperation should aim to make the disciplined, government-controlled ISF units the "first among equals" and, over time, the dominant military power inside Iraq. It is an achievable aim, particularly if undertaken steadily and in a sustained manner. Although a raw man-for-man comparison shows the Iran-backed PMF and Badr units of the Ministry of Interior holding a rough parity with the Iraqi army and CTS units,[4] the latter pro-government forces are gaining ground in training, continuous combat experience, and adequately maintained heavy equipment (see Annex B). Furthermore, if and when decisive clashes happen between Iran-controlled and loyalist ISF, those clashes probably will not involve full mobilization of all sides but rather will involve large skirmishes of each side's praetorian units. Already, the loyalist ISF faces down the militias when ordered to do so, even if it is always a close contest. International Zone security forces of the CTS and Iraqi army effectively protected the seat of government on May 26, 2021, in a messy, but ultimately successful, pushback against militia efforts to enter the zone in strength. Numerous successful arrests of militiamen have been made by praetorian ISF special forces, even if the judiciary has later released the suspects. These indicators show growing confidence and firmness by the ISF when it is led well from the prime minister down.

Reasonable U.S. Expectations

The United States remains a superb, sought-after security partner, but the country's expectations can be out of touch with reality and with the objectives of partner forces. For instance, in Congress's quarterly reports on Operation Inherent Resolve, a kind of mania can be detected regarding the belief that Iraq must develop a technologically sophisticated reconnaissance-strike complex that resembles how America undertakes counterinsurgency and counterterrorism across the world. ISF eventually being able to construct the perfect "kill chain" may have become the U.S. idea of success—in effect, handing off U.S. missions to a clone of the United States—but it is far from what is achievable at this point, nor should it be the U.S. metric for success.

Instead, there are immediate issues and achievable outcomes that the United States can justifiably identify as desirable, as well as necessary changes in the operating environment. These gains might form the basis for loose conditionality to continue *some* U.S. assistance—not holding the entire security cooperation relationship at risk, but perhaps some premium parts of the package (such as a portion of funding, or no-cost or low-cost granting of Excess Defense Articles, or sensitive and sought-after technology transfers and intelligence sharing). Reasonable U.S. expectations include the following:

- **Reduced security threat to U.S. advisors.** The threat to U.S. and coalition forces in Iraq must reduce reasonably quickly. Congress's Inspector General confirms that the U.S. government counted twenty rocket and drone attacks on U.S. sites in the first half of 2021 and seventy-eight roadside bomb attacks on logistical convoys supporting the U.S presence.[5] The number of roadside bombs against such convoys are less material to the United States as no U.S. persons are present on such convoys, but indirect fire attacks on U.S. points of presence and kidnap threats are a serious concern. Continuous downward trending in the number of such attacks should be a prerequisite for the release of premium elements of the security cooperation package.

- **Less diversion of U.S. aid.** The risk of diversion of U.S. aid must also reduce very rapidly, and ideally in the 2022 Iraqi budget. In particular, the United States has every right, as the largest security cooperation provider to Iraq, to expect that Iraq's defense and security budget is well managed. Thus, the budgets of the Ministry of Defense and CTS must be protected from predation by other security agencies. In the 2021 budget, for instance, the Ministry of Defense suffered a 25.6 percent decrease in its funds and CTS lost 19.9 percent of funding, while the PMF saw a 17 percent increase in its budget.[6] In effect, U.S. security assistance created space for the diversion of Defense Ministry and CTS funding to the PMF, which is absolutely *not* the intended effect of U.S. support. The trend of growing PMF funding at the expense of Defense Ministry and CTS procurement and sustainment needs to stop. The United States and other security assistance providers should place conditions on some aid that future cuts to Iraqi defense spending would be applied more evenly.

- **Improved Baghdad-Kurdistan and intra-Kurdish synergies.** Domestic cooperation and deconfliction between Iraqi agencies—especially with the Peshmerga—must improve meaningfully and within a short timeframe. At present (as figure 1.4 showed), the United States can point to multiple gross inefficiencies in federal-Kurdish and intra-Kurdish security arrangements. First, regarding the Kurdistan Control Line, federal and Kurdish forces are arrayed against each other along a 590-kilometer internal frontier, not against IS, and these ISF units cannot move fluidly where they are needed. Second, the two main

Kurdish parties—the Kurdistan Democratic Party (KDP) and Patriotic Union of Kurdistan (PUK)—operate armed forces that are too large and duplicative, and which do not cooperate fully. Third, due to federal-Kurdish revenue-sharing disputes, Baghdad has persistently refused to pay a portion of the Peshmerga, which has resulted in America allocating $17–$20 million per month to cover their salaries.[7] This is clearly not a position the United States should accept open-endedly. Comprehensive integration of Kurdistan Region security forces via milestones and measures of progress is a reasonable U.S. expectation.

- **Focus of human rights and anti-corruption.** Human rights and anti-corruption concerns must be addressed more seriously. The United States does not look hard enough for evidence of human rights abusers and corrupt commanders within services and units that it supports, often terming the exercise "sheep-dipping" (i.e., a quick check for problems and a clean bill of health). As America shifts to supporting the whole ISF enterprise at a higher level, U.S. officials should expect and review measurable progress in Iraq's weeding out of human rights abusers and corrupt officers from its command cadres. This effort should include all Iraqi officers who order the use of lethal force on unarmed protestors or who carry out such orders.

Notes

1   Author interviews, multiple U.S. contacts, 2019–2020 (exact dates, names, and places withheld at request of interviewees).

2   Michael Knights, *How to Secure Mosul: Lessons from 2008–2014*, Policy Note 38 (Washington DC: Washington Institute, 2016), 2, https://www.washingtoninstitute.org/policy-analysis/how-secure-mosul-lessons-2008-2014.

3   Office of the Special Inspector for Iraq Reconstruction (SIGIR), "Iraqi Special Operations Forces Program Is Achieving Goals, but Iraqi Support Remains Critical to Success," SIGIR, October 25, 2010, 12, https://apps.dtic.mil/sti/citations/ADA545722.

4   Michael Knights, "Iran's Expanding Militia Army in Iraq: The New Special Groups," *CTC Sentinel* 12, no. 7 (2019), https://ctc.usma.edu/irans-expanding-militia-army-iraq-new-special-groups/.

5   "Operation Inherent Resolve Quarterly Report, April 1–June 30, 2021," 44–46.

6   Ibid., xx.

7   Ibid., 37.

3

Road Map for Future Security Cooperation

On December 31, 2021, the U.S.-led coalition in Iraq will undergo a formal "transition of mission" to a non-combat, operational-level advise and assist effort. The coalition is essentially already at this stage, but the deadline underlines the change in a way that will hopefully be widely recognized and accepted within Iraq and within Washington. With small adjustments to force posture, one chapter of the U.S.-led security cooperation in Iraq will end and another will begin. What should the new chapter look like?

Sustain the U.S.-Led Military Safety Net

Iran-backed militias in Iraq will not readily accept an ongoing presence of U.S.-led coalition forces in Iraq in 2022. They are anticipating, at best, humiliating the United States and the ISF by physically taking over and looting current U.S. facilities such as the coalition compounds within al-Asad Air Base and Baghdad International Airport. In late 2021, as the December 31 deadline looms, the Iraqi government will probably still be locked in post-election "government formation" (i.e., selecting a prime minister and cabinet) and Prime Minister Kadhimi's government will be in caretaker status. Such militias will probably try to rattle the transitioning Iraqi government with the threat of violence—and violence itself—into seeking an actual drawdown of remaining international advisors and the removal from Iraq of U.S. "enablers" of the ISF (e.g., drones, ISR aircraft, and special forces advisors). The shutting down of Iraqi airspace to all U.S. aircraft would be welcomed by militias, which fear that such assets could be used against them, unilaterally by the United States or in partnership with the Iraqi state, particularly in scenarios where militias pose a coup risk to the elected Iraqi government. At the very least, creating the expectation of U.S. withdrawal, followed by no real change in the level of presence, would help militias sustain their "resistance" narrative against what they characterize as "foreign occupation."

The U.S. government should take proactive steps to reduce the risk of an eviction crisis. The transition of mission to a "non-combat" operation for all Iraq-based forces should be advertised, and the clearest distinction visible to Iraqis would be the end of all U.S. kinetic operations inside Iraq. Already, U.S. troops based in Iraq do not conduct combat missions in the country: the small remaining number of special operators advise the ISF but do not undertake combat operations inside Iraq. Nor do U.S. armed drones based in Iraq need to conduct airstrikes within the country, except when the United States is conducting self-defense. Any ongoing airstrikes requested by the Iraqi government, should the United States wish to accommodate such rare requests, can be serviced by U.S. aircraft and armed drones based outside Iraq. The U.S. military currently strikes inside Iraq only about seven times a month, so this number can decline without serious negative impact on ISF operations. The end of the 2002 Authorization of the Use of Military Force in Iraq, when it comes, should not present a problem.[1] As in Jordan or Kuwait, where there is no AUMF but also no use of force, the normalization of the U.S.-led coalition military presence in Iraq is easily achievable. In the case of severe emergencies, Iraq can always request ad hoc military support under new U.S. and Iraqi authorities.[2]

If the U.S. president is forced to undertake self-defense actions against militias, they should largely be taken outside Iraq (i.e., in Syria or Iran). If strikes must occur inside Iraq, the actions might at first use warning strikes (like Israeli "roof knocking") to achieve close misses or let personnel escape before destroying materiel, and the United States should not publicly discuss or confirm its involvement in such actions.[3] These types of actions will help the moderate majority in Iraq's parliament avoid pressure such as it felt on January 7, 2020, when a sizable minority of MPs (though without a legal quorum) managed to bring a parliamentary motion to remove foreign forces.

Recognize and Publicize the Risks of Full Withdrawal

Although the U.S. military does not buttress the ISF in the same manner that the ANSF relied on U.S. forces in Afghanistan[4] or Yemeni forces rely on Saudi airpower against Houthi offensives,[5] there would nonetheless be very negative outcomes for U.S. interests if Iraqis perceived themselves to have been abandoned by the U.S.-led coalition. The results would not be as rapid or dramatic as those in Afghanistan, where the February 2020 withdrawal agreement triggered more than a year of Taliban preparation for a takeover and then a remarkably swift conquest of most government-controlled areas in little more than a month. In Iraq, the model would more likely be Iraq's own security deterioration in 2012–14, perhaps even a slower variant, but would nonetheless reverse progress in ISF development, encourage IS and Iran-backed militias, and accelerate the breakdown of ISF processes and contractor support. Invisible and insidious deterioration would begin to dissolve ISF morale and institutions. Within five years, Iraq would likely be back on the path toward chronic insecurity, as opposed to its present trajectory of tentative recovery.

Politicians in Baghdad and Washington must clearly understand ahead of December 31, 2021, that a full coalition departure from Iraq would be quite disastrous for the broader international presence in, and support to, Iraq and Syria. Without the logistics and force protection assets of the coalition, most of which are contributed by the United States, it would be hard for many entities, most notably the following, to remain in Iraq and Syria:

- **U.S. and international diplomatic presence.** The U.S. embassy in Baghdad was almost overrun by armed militias on December 31, 2019.

The embassy and the U.S. consulate in Erbil rely upon the primarily U.S. forces and assets of the coalition for force protection, hospital facilities, logistics, and evacuation assurance via the coalition sides of Baghdad and Erbil airports. If the U.S. diplomatic corps were forced to leave Iraq, many other nations would also leave. These departures would cede the ground in Iraq to Iran, Russia, and China.

- **NATO in Iraq.** Without coalition support, NATO Mission Iraq (NMI) would also lack the life support and guard forces to operate in its current premises, the Union III base in Baghdad. Although the North Atlantic Council authorized NMI to prepare for self-sustainment, NMI is still very early in planning how to implement it.

- **Coalition forces in Syria.** U.S. forces at al-Asad Air Base are needed to protect transiting logistics flights, U.S. ISR aircraft, and training facilities, and they provide support and assured evacuation to the U.S. garrison at al-Tanf in Syria. The U.S. facility at Erbil International Airport supports U.S. diplomats and coalition presence at the Kurdistan Military Training Center. The Harir Air Base in the Kurdistan Region of Iraq provides vital air and special forces support to the ISF and counter-IS forces in Syria. U.S. operating locations in Kurdistan provide a secure line of supply and line of evacuation for U.S. forces in northeast Syria.

Explain that International Presence Is at Its Minimum Viable Level

There are many good reasons to argue for the maintenance of the coalition presence in Iraq for another year or two and to reason that Combined Joint Task Force–Operation Inherent Resolve (CJTF-OIR) has arguably reached an irreducible minimum size in Iraq. The mix of U.S. and non-U.S. forces, however, could alter, as could the balance of CJTF-OIR and NATO-badged troops. In terms of raw numbers, the 2,500 U.S. troops in Iraq, plus up to a thousand other coalition forces, represent the minimal viable force manning to support a range of U.S. and partner government actions in Iraq.

As noted previously, U.S. forces present under the rubric of the coalition currently operate the logistics of international presence in Baghdad, as well as counter-rocket and missile and counter-drone defenses in Baghdad and other sites. U.S. ISR assets not only operate under the coalition, keeping a watchful eye on IS, but also ensure force protection for the coalition, contractors, and diplomatic quarter in Baghdad. The Baghdad Diplomatic Support Center inside Baghdad International Airport must remain to support U.S. ISR aircraft, the Baghdad embassy, special forces advisors at Iraq's Area IV academy, NATO, and the coalition's thirteen-nation Military Advisory Group (MAG) at Union III. Interestingly, if the militia threat to coalition personnel did not exist, the number of foreign troops could reduce significantly, meaning that the militias themselves hold coalition forces at their current levels.

It would seem risky to diminish the coalition's mandate, resources, or profile—symbols of continuity in international support for Iraq—at a time when Iraqi military confidence has not hardened and when the memory of U.S. withdrawal from Afghanistan is fresh. As long as the Iraqi government continues to extend its invitation to international advisors in 2022–23, the U.S.-led coalition should stay at roughly the current levels (2,500 troops) to signal steadiness and reassurance to Iraq and America's coalition partners. This is not a case of leaving U.S. persons in harm's way merely to avoid the inevitable end of a lost cause, as the U.S. government now characterizes Afghanistan, but rather to cement gains in Iraq, where the heavy lifting is finished and where U.S.-led military support has already helped Iraq *succeed* against the Islamic State. U.S. persons do still face threats in Iraq—there have been two U.S. military deaths and two U.S. citizen contractor deaths in Iraqi in the past twenty months[6] —but it is important for U.S. adversaries (from Great Power competitors to terrorist groups) to understand that they cannot drive America out of strategic relationships by killing American diplomats and trainers. If America is shown to be a "giant with clay feet," it will only encourage more attacks on Americans wherever enemies seek to drive them out.

Transition Some Activities to NATO and Other Partners, 2022–23

By 2024, CJTF-OIR may well have run its course, having demonstrably achieved its mission. At that point, today's mainly-U.S. coalition effort should probably be split across two interconnected lines of effort—bilateral U.S.-Iraq security cooperation and NATO. In 2019–20, when the issue of sudden U.S. withdrawal was urgently relevant, it seemed wishful to imagine that the tiny 500-person NATO Mission Iraq (NMI) presence could scale up to perform the range of tasks being undertaken by the 5,000-strong U.S.-led coalition force in Iraq. However, over a longer timeframe, servicing tomorrow's non-combat requirements, an enhanced NMI role could be far more credible if NATO can apply some of the practical lessons of the six-year NATO-led Resolute Support Mission in Afghanistan regarding funding efficiencies and streamlined processes.

Backed by an extant Iraqi/NATO exchange of letters and North Atlantic Council authorization, NMI is now willing and appropriately authorized to expand its support to the ISF and Iraqi security institutions in the coming years. Indeed, NATO's robust exchange of letters since 2016 with three successive Iraqi prime ministers resulted in 2021 in NATO Mission Iraq being accorded full diplomatic status, privileges, immunities, and facilities in accordance with the Vienna Convention on Diplomatic Relations of April 18, 1961. NATO currently lacks funding and equipment, both of which the United States is in a position to divest as CJTF-OIR ramps down. Importantly, NMI is likely to have access to the larger numbers of U.S. and non-U.S. advisors needed to develop long-term, persistent relationships within the Iraqi security ministries and uniformed ISF (see figure 3.1).

Working through the newly streamlined High Committee on Security Sector Reform, which is overseen by the Office of the Prime Minister, NATO is one of a number of actors feeding into a synergized program of security sector reform, others being the European Union Advisory Mission–Iraq (EUAM-I), the UN Development Programme, the Defense Security Cooperation Agency's Institute for Security Governance,[7] U.S. Office of Security

Figure 3.1. Iraq's Multinational Security Sector Pantheon

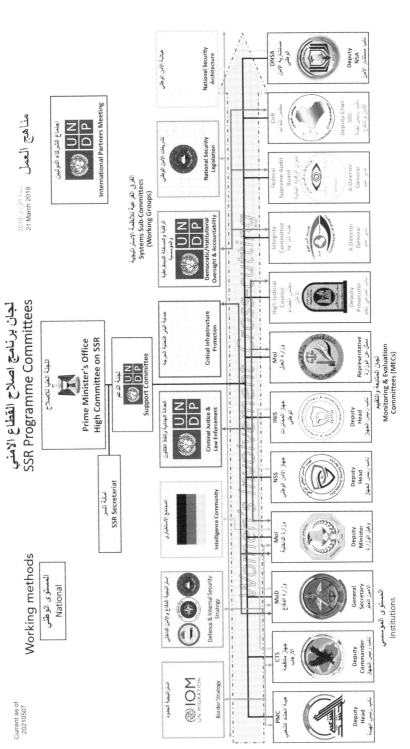

Diagram used with permission of NATO.

Cooperation–Iraq, Britain, and Germany. Non-U.S. partners—which the United States terms "unified action partners" in such joint efforts—are vital force multipliers. European work on intelligence community training and reforms has been quiet and effective. Although stalled in the design phase for more than six months, EUAM-I and the U.S. International Organization for Migration are now working with the Ministry of Interior on an Integrated Border Management Strategy. A future multinational effort could be the cooperative development of organic Iraqi defense logistics, maintenance, overhaul, and licensed spare parts industries, as envisaged in Iraq's Defense Manufacturing Law (Law No. 25 of 2019).[8]

Key NATO Focus Areas

NMI currently advises on institutional development at the Prime Minister–National Operations Center (PM-NOC), Iraqi Office of the National Security Advisor (ONSA), and Ministry of Defense at ministerial, secretary-general, and chief of defense staff levels, plus their deputies. In the first phase of expanded engagement in 2022, NMI has been invited by Iraq to advise individual service branches (Iraqi Ground Forces Command, Iraqi Air Defense Command, Iraqi Naval Forces Command, Iraqi Air Defense Forces, and Iraqi Army Aviation Command) within the Defense Ministry, followed by other ministries (Ministry of Interior, in partnership with EUAM-I) and the Ministry of Peshmerga Affairs in the Kurdistan Region.

NMI is most effective when it does not seek to eliminate any fiefdoms too rapidly and obviously but instead focuses on steady improvements.[9] Key NMI-supported initiatives that are steadily unfolding or are planned include the following:

- **Policy and strategy.** NMI and other partners are helping Iraq update its foundational National Security Strategy and National Defense Strategy documents. Unlike previous iterations, forthcoming strategy documents should incorporate the Kurdistan Region fully.

- **Force structure planning.** NMI and the Office of Security Cooperation–Iraq (OSC-I) are partnering with the Defense Ministry to facilitate workshops and mentoring the ministry for defining requirements, allocating resources, and identifying gaps to assess current force structure and what force structure changes are necessary for missions, tasks, and functions of the ministry looking ahead.

- **Force generation.**
  - » *Training syllabi updates.* Iraq has requested that NMI provide updates to the Defense Ministry training syllabi at the Iraqi Centralized Training Facility (CTF) in Taji. In time, this could expand to the other four CTFs at al-Taqqadum, Camp Dublin, Bismayah, and the Kurdistan Training Coordination Center.
  - » *Logistics management policies and systems.* This initiative with the Defense Ministry M4 (logistics) branch will improve and automate the procurement of spare parts and other maintenance improvements. NMI could finally help Iraq develop a partially automated spare parts inventory and supply chain system.
  - » *Readiness workshops.* This initiative with Defense Ministry M7 (training), the ministry's Readiness Office, and its security reform committee will develop a reset system and schedule for ISF units to rotate through CTFs.
  - » *Professional military education.* This initiative includes further development of officer training at Rustamiyah academy and other military education institutions in Baghdad. The Defense Language Institute should be boosted in size and capacity, to reverse the current decline of English-language fluency across the ISF, which particularly affects procurement and technical branches.

- **Human resource management system.** This work currently involves the Defense Ministry. (The Ministry of Peshmerga Affairs is provided some human resource management systems and training by OSC-I.) This support may be expanded to the Counter Terrorism Service and Interior Ministry, including the Department of Border Enforcement.
  - » *Performance and career monitoring.* This effort would enable performance and career monitoring, ensuring that personnel are placed

in jobs that match and further develop their skills and experience.

» ***Right-sizing and fraud reduction.*** It would also support audit of ISF personnel numbers and pensions, fraud reduction, and manpower optimization. Iraq's effective strength is presently too low, but its establishment strength (and salary budget) is too high because of the "ghost soldier" phenomenon of fraudulent registration of part-time or nonexistent personnel.

» ***Off-ramp for former soldiers.*** NMI can also help Iraq ensure that redundant ISF members (including Popular Mobilization Forces) are encouraged to separate from the ISF—with vocational training and new business microgrants—into legitimate private-sector occupations as opposed to militia or criminal movements.

- **ISF medical care systems.** The Defense Ministry has long sought foreign assistance to build an ISF hospital with effective casualty evacuation capabilities, which would not start from scratch but rather draw together many disparate capabilities and weave them together, along with injections of new equipment and training. The experience of U.S. development of field surgical hospitals in Syria demonstrates that medical services are among the most needed and appreciated type of security cooperation that the United States can provide to partner forces.[10]

Expanded NATO Footprint

These kinds of capacity-building efforts are exactly what the ISF needs to overcome its observed weaknesses in professionalism, leadership, planning, readiness, and sustainment. As such programs unfold according to expressed Iraqi requirements, they will require expanded manning, from the current levels of under six hundred NMI personnel in Iraq to three or four times that number by 2023, depending on exact Iraqi requirements.[11] Civilian advisors will be in especially high demand, to even out the current imbalance toward uniformed advisors and to bring in the requisite skill-sets. (These include civilian oversight and governance of the armed forces, international security partnerships, programming, planning, budgeting, procurement and execution oversight, ministerial-level direction and guidance, prioritization of finite resources application to meet overall security objectives, and recruitment, pay, and retention.)

To fit in more personnel, NMI will require more space—within the existing CJTF-OIR basing structure to avoid new building costs—plus life support and base protection, including counter-missile/rocket/drone systems. The obvious solution is to plan out a slow transition of U.S. personnel and equipment from their present badging under CJTF-OIR to new badging under NMI. Eventually NMI could take over many of the "care and feeding" and base defense responsibilities of today's CJTF-OIR, initially with the same level of U.S. contribution of personnel and funding but eventually with a more diverse set of contributors. The United States is one of the few nations that could provide sufficient civilian advisors in the midst of a fragile security environment to allow NMI to operate effectively. The United States could ensure that its contribution is counted against its contribution to NATO.

Optimize Bilateral U.S.-Iraq Security Cooperation

The eventual phaseout of CJTF-OIR will be year zero for a new epoch of U.S.-Iraq security cooperation and strategic relations. This era would not be a time of invasion and state-building (2003–11), nor the defeat of IS (since 2014), but rather something new. It would be the inception of a fresh effort, not a contingency operation but a normalized steady state, a regular condition-based sustained partnership without an end point or exit strategy. A new vision needs to undergird this new era. The vison for the non-combat U.S. role should not be based on old authorizations from contingency operations, such as the defunct 2002 Authorization for the Use of Military Force in Iraq, nor the aging post-9/11 AUMF from 2001.

Foreign Internal Defense Focus

Rather than reinventing the wheel, the United States might draw upon and adapt the U.S. military concept of foreign internal defense (FID), which envisages: "Programs or activities taken by a host nation government to free and protect its society from subversion, lawlessness, insurgency, violent extremism, terrorism and other threats to its security."[12]

FID is typically conducted by special forces, often under Department of State oversight and authorities, with support from a whole-of-government interagency process.[13] Foreign internal defense stresses *non-combat* operations such as "indirect support" (strengthening host nation security institutions) and "direct support not involving combat operations" (e.g., as-needed provision of U.S. ISR or logistical support). FID tends to stress the minimization of the use of force and the strengthening of host nation institutions and internal defense capabilities. FID is appropriate for "other than normal" security cooperation environments in which security risk may be elevated.

The basic approach of FID seems very suitable to Iraq, albeit in a modified form. Security cooperation in Iraq is going to be conducted in an "other than normal" force protection environment for many years, necessitating higher risk acceptance and an expeditionary mindset more usual to FID operations than traditional security cooperation arrangements. The United States is not aiming to prepare Iraq for interstate conflict against its neighbors, and neither Iraq nor the United States has the resources to support such an effort in any case. Foreign Internal Defense is also a useful concept because it normalizes security cooperation outside the confines of the specific counter-IS contingency. The Islamic State is not the only danger, and perhaps not the main one, that Iraq will face in the future.

If Iraq transitions into a more normal relationship with the United States—akin to the U.S.-Jordan security relationship—then U.S. security cooperation also should normalize to address the full range of security needs identified by the Iraqi government. U.S. Special Forces may indeed play an outsize role in a FID-type engagement in Iraq, but (as the following sections will note) U.S. support to Iraq would clearly not be limited to a special forces–led FID effort. Many other instruments of U.S. national power would also be used (see figure 3.2).

Jordan: The Model for U.S.-Iraq Cooperation

Jordan should be the model for future U.S.-Iraq cooperation. Aside from Title 50 operations that are intelligence or covert activities, Jordan receives a mix of Title 22 security assistance under a State Department lead and Title 10 security cooperation assistance under a Defense Department lead. As the State Department notes, "Jordan's stability and security are priorities for the United States" and America is committed to strengthening Jordanian security forces without the identification of any particular enemy against which that the support is focused.[14] Memorialized in a series of nonbinding multiyear MOUs,[15] U.S. security cooperation is planned out in multiyear blocks, e.g., the intention to provide a minimum of $350 million of Foreign Military Financing to Jordan each year).[16]

This multiyear approach represents a U.S. commitment to long-term support, which in turn can encourage reform and the cohesive building of capabilities using multi-budget (as opposed to year-on-year) funding. Like Iraq, Jordan is one of the largest global accounts with the FMF and Foreign Military Sales (FMS) systems.[17] Like Iraq, Jordan uses general (Section 333) and country-specific tailored U.S. security cooperation programs (e.g., the $234 million Jordan Border Security Program).[18] Jordan has sent more than six thousand officers through U.S. professional military education in the United States through International Military Training and Education funding, creating broad and deep cultural ties to the United States and relationships across the Jordanian Armed Forces. The U.S. mission in Jordan is low profile yet surprisingly large and is a model for America and Iraq to aspire to. The coalition is already adopting U.S.-style nomenclature (Military Advisory Group-Iraq or MAG-I, similar to MAG-J in Jordan), a pointer toward the coming evolution.

Jordan is a particularly suitable model because some kind of special bilateral arrangement is needed to gently transition Iraq from the massive contingency security cooperation of the counter-IS war to the traditional security cooperation relationship that will exist after 2023, when CJTF-OIR will most likely to expire. Congress needs to understand that while funds do not need to match CTEF dollar for dollar, Iraq should be weaned off CTEF

Figure 3.2. The Security Cooperation Landscape in Iraq

Currently, U.S. security cooperation to Iraq is provided via a range of different security cooperation organizations. The diagram that follows shows the range of mechanisms used by the United States and partner nations to administer security cooperation with the ISF. For an explanation of the different types of aid, see the table in Annex A.

- **U.S. Title 22** programs are run by the State Department and either fully administered by the State Department from Washington and the U.S. embassy or consulate in Iraq, or operated in coordination with the Defense Department through the Office of Security Cooperation–Iraq (OSC-I).[a]

- **U.S. Title 10** encompasses Defense Department–run military operations such as those undertaken by U.S. forces in Combined Joint Task Force–Operation Inherent Resolve.

- Some U.S. defense budget–funded security cooperation programs—e.g., Counter-IS Train and Equip Fund, Excess Defense Articles, and Sections 127e, 333, and 1206—are jointly administered by the State and Defense Departments, with the former coauthorizing them and military institutions implementing them.[b]

- **U.S. Title 50** operations are covert operations not covered in this study.

- International partners are executing their own security cooperation in partnership with the ISF, separate from U.S. efforts but with potential synergies.

---

[a]RAND notes: "Title 22 funds are appropriated to the State Department, which often transfers them to DOD, which in turn manages and executes most security assistance programs. Title 22 includes Foreign Military Sales programs. Title 22 is less flexible in some ways, mainly because Congress authorizes and appropriates these funds on a by-country and by-program basis, and requires congressional notification and permission to move funds from one effort to another." See Terrence K. Kelly et al., *Security Cooperation Organizations in the Country Team: Options for Success* (RAND, 2010), xii, at https://www.rand.org/content/dam/rand/pubs/technical_reports/2010/RAND_TR734.sum.pdf.

[b]RAND notes: "Title 10 funds are appropriated to the Defense Department and are intended for operations and maintenance of the U.S. military. These funds are often used to fund international participation in U.S. joint exercises, military personnel exchanges, or military-to-military contacts as a way to enhance the relationships between partner militaries and U.S. forces." See Terrence K. Kelly et al., "Security Cooperation Organizations in the Country Team: Options for Success," (RAND, 2010), xii, https://www.rand.org/content/dam/rand/pubs/technical_reports/2010/RAND_TR734.sum.pdf.

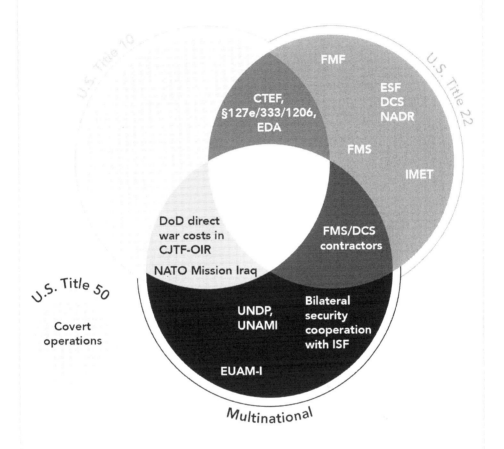

CTEF	Counter-IS Train and Equip Fund
DCS	Direct Combat Support
ESF	Emergency Support Fund
EUAM-I	European Union Advisory Mission–Iraq
FMF	Foreign Military Financing
FMS	Foreign Military Sales
ISF	Iraqi security forces
NADR	Nonproliferation, Antiterrorism, Demining, and Related (programs)
UNAMI	United Nations Assistance Mission for Iraq
UNDP	United Nations Development Programme

in a gradual way before becoming mainly reliant on traditional security cooperation tools, such as FMS and FMF. Title 10 support tools such as CTEF make the divestment of equipment quick and flexible, while Title 22 traditional tools (like FMS and FMF) are slower and more administratively cumbersome. CTEF needs to be replaced with some kind of Iraq carve-out within a global fund such as Section 333 funding (e.g., the Jordan Operational Engagement Program, or JOEP)[19] or via a country-specific FMF mechanism that emerges as a new section of code in the U.S. defense budget (e.g., the Jordan Border Security Program).[20]

Developing a Multiyear Security Cooperation Plan

As in Jordan, where multiyear plans underpin the relationship, Iraq and the United States need to begin with a foundational road map that comprises identified destinations, milestones, and waypoints. The longer a joint plan can be, the better for acquisition planning: five years at a minimum, but ideally ten years, to enable efficient long-term planning and budgeting processes. A joint strategic review process at the Prime Minister's Office level needs to lay out a multiyear, multi-budget plan for Iraqi internal defense requirements, including established roles and missions for the different security forces and a force structure review. This review is vital for a range of reasons. First, it will create a baseline for rightsizing and restructuring the ISF so that it better fits the task set and also Iraq's tightening budget resources. Second, the identification of roles and missions for all the ISF— including the PMF—is critical for the redeployment of forces and the reduction of duplication of roles (e.g., the redundant layering of army, border, and PMF forces in many areas). In some areas, the need for new or consolidated units may be identified, such as the folding-in of Kurdistan Region units or personnel into Iraqi formations such as CTS or joint commands along the Kurdistan Control Line. For the first time, Iraq will have defined roles and missions (and thus budgeting and deployment guidance) for forces such as the Federal Police and the PMF. Third, such a process will make international support easier—for instance, by gaining a clear understanding of how Iraqi ministries share responsibilities for critical infrastructure protection.

Iraq must set aside sufficient funding for agreed projects and meet certain conditions (see following sections) in order to receive the support contained within each part of the security cooperation plan. Specific Iraqi commitments to time-tabled objectives and programs might include the following:

- Protect Defense Ministry and CTS budgets from disproportionate reductions vis-à-vis the PMF's rising budget.
- Demonstrate positive trajectory on leadership, training, and sustainment through ministerial capacity building.
- Complete internal redeployment of Iraqi military manpower, including Baghdad-Kurdistan efforts to achieve sufficient force density along the Kurdistan Control Line.
- Support population-focused counterinsurgency in remaining IS hotspots that stresses the return of internally displaced persons, human rights, and counterinsurgency training, and the incorporation of local security forces into police formations.
- Facilitate border security milestones on the Syrian, Turkish, and Iranian borders, including demonstrated primacy for Department of Border Enforcement troops and removal of PMF units.

Iraq should also initiate self-funding of some security cooperation efforts as a demonstration of commitment and as part of a partnership funding agreement. This expenditure would ensure Iraq was forced to make difficult prioritization decisions. If Iraq can make such commitments, then not only the United States but also deep-pocketed supporters (like Saudi Arabia and the UAE) might be encouraged to make larger and longer-term commitments within the framework of a Security Sector Reform Trust Fund. For instance, Gulf state sponsors might be ideal for undertaking infrastructure development at Iraqi bases and for the divestment of (barely) used military equipment and spare parts. Donations would be pooled, with earmarking of funds to reflect the national interests of donors (e.g., women's issues, peace and security, policing counterterrorism). The fund would activate projects on the basis of a formula of matching Iraqi and international funding.

OSC-I and Other Bilateral Programs

In 2022–23, most of the remaining U.S. functions of CJTF-OIR that are not adopted by NATO could be folded within the U.S. embassy-based Office of Security Cooperation–Iraq or a rebadged security cooperation office. In particular, the value of U.S. procurement support cannot be overstated in a case like Iraq's. As the earlier discussion of the low serviceability of Russian and Chinese aerial platforms noted,[21] with the exception of those supported by the United States, these non-U.S. systems are orphaned soon after they are sold to Iraq, with little thought to sustainable provision of spare parts. The U.S. FMS system is the opposite: not a shortsighted and corrupt way for officials to make illegal commissions, as is often the case with Russian and Chinese cases, but an enduring commitment to support systems, even though the administrative burden of processing sales is assumed by the United States. Iraq must be encouraged to take the long view on strategic partnerships. Already, evidence of that view is showing in the Iraqi Ministry of Oil's fear of overreliance on lower-quality Russian and Chinese companies whose approach is short term, damaging to Iraq's oil reservoirs, and often more expensive than Western firms over the life cycle of projects. This kind of long view is growing in the Iraqi security sector, too, and is the basis for significant competitive advantage for the United States as a partner.

OSC-I or a successor will remain a vital tool in future U.S. security cooperation because of the large-scale ongoing FMS, FMF, and other Title 22 programs that need to be managed in Iraq, which include $16.3 billion in active government-to-government sales cases.[22] As important, an expanded embassy-based security cooperation office can help to shape the "demand signal" from Iraq and assist in the design of ongoing acquisition and development strategy. Until Iraq's Defense Language Institute is able to ramp up English tuition for procurement officers, OSC-I will have to provide extensive support to the writing of Iraqi letters of requirement. To achieve U.S. objectives, therefore, OSC-I needs to increase its paltry funding (currently just $25 million requested in FY2022) and the dedicated or allocated security resources to leave the embassy to visit Iraqi defense sites and liaise more closely with Iraqi defense leaders.

There is also an argument for transferring U.S. support to the Ministry of Peshmerga Affairs out of the declining U.S. Counter-IS Train and Equip Fund and into a specialized bilateral fund such as Section 333 (Authority to Build Capacity) of the U.S. defense budget. The Peshmerga stipends are unique, with no other security force in Iraq receiving such treatment, and the funding is not, in reality, directly tied to counter-IS operations but rather used as leverage to drive Peshmerga reunification and reform processes. NMI is unlikely to take on Peshmerga reform as a core task. There are already many bilateral security cooperation engagements with the Ministry of Peshmerga Affairs; NMI would need to establish new sites in the Kurdistan Region of Iraq; and NMI would need a new specific request from the Iraqi government to extend into Kurdistan. In working in the Kurdistan Region, the Turkish component of NMI would be a complicating factor. (As the authors have experienced, NMI cannot even use the correct term "Kurdistan Regional Government" and must, by Turkish requirement, use the incorrect "Kurdish Regional Government" to avoid recognizing a "Kurdistan.") As a result, NMI may face an uphill struggle to work in Kurdistan, and the United States, alongside partners like Britain, should develop a specific bilateral program with the Ministry of Peshmerga Affairs.

Finally, as in Jordan, the United States should arrange regular joint exercise programs with Iraq to signal U.S. rotating and nonpermanent presence, but also its enduring relationships, engagement, and commitment. Presently, U.S. support to Iraqi special forces is split across coalition programs (with CTS and, in prior years, the Ministry of Interior's Emergency Response Division), U.S. Title 22 funding (with Defense Ministry commando units known as *quwat khasa*, or QK), and Title 50 operations. To synchronize these efforts, U.S. Central Command should develop similar special forces training programs to those that exist with the King Abdullah II Special Operations Training Center (KASOTC) in Jordan, potentially in partnership with KASOTC itself, which has a close relationship with Iraq's Ministry of Defense.

Central Command could initially hold small special forces and air force training exercises inside Iraq multiple times per year. If carefully built around the adapting threat from IS or other domestic adversaries, such exercises might help Iraq develop counterinsurgency approaches such as night operations, ambushes, air/artillery and ISR integration, and support to local special forces, including local SWAT teams and the commando units of Iraqi brigades and divisions. Initially, the United States should negotiate access and protections for such exercises on a case-by-case basis. Eventually, if Iraq stabilizes and becomes familiar with a normalized security relationship, it may be possible to develop more formal Status of Forces and Acquisition and Cross-Servicing agreements, and later a structure similar to the 2021 U.S.-Jordan Defense Cooperation Agreement. Optimistically, the United States and Iraq should envision small exercises growing into larger annual exercises and eventually also biennial large-scale exercises that might involve regional states (akin to the U.S.-Egypt Bright Star exercises).

Principles to Guide Future U.S. Security Cooperation with Iraq

U.S.-Iraq security cooperation has been dominated for most of the post-2003 period by contingency arrangements, driven by urgent operational conditions and understandable impatience by the United States to downsize its presence in Iraq. Going forward, the U.S. executive branch, military, and Congress need to adapt their mindsets as the relationship normalizes and moves beyond contingency thinking. The United States and Iraq should pursue an open-ended security cooperation relationship that is not contingent on any particular tactical goal or specific adversary (such as the enduring defeat of IS). The U.S. security relationship with Jordan is rooted in Washington's desire to see the kingdom succeed and remain stable, and the same objectives and outlook should be applied to Iraq. U.S. multiyear, multi-budget plans for engagement with Iraq should stress longevity and enduring commitment at sustainable levels, commensurate with U.S. interests.

With NATO Mission Iraq ideally leading on broader security sector reform and professionalization of the entire ISF enterprise, U.S. bilateral partnership should be parsimonious and focus on building very strong, relatively narrow relationships with certain parts of the ISF. This longevity and focus are how the United States succeeded in inculcating high levels of professionalism in the CTS, by growing the young Iraqi special forces lieutenants of 2004 into the Iraqi colonels of 2021. In partnership with CTS and other U.S.-supported special forces (*quwat khasa*, or QK), a specialized counterinsurgency advise and assist effort (to replace the coalition Special Operations Advisor Group) could help Iraq sustain its counter-IS effort during what could be a slow, drawn-out eclipse of Islamic State cells in the liberated areas. These forces—along with select Iraqi army armor units—also provide Iraq with a counter-coup capability that has already been exercised in this role once in 2021.[23] Above all, Iraq needs a diamond-hard counter-coup force, built around QK, the CTS, and armored forces, to defend the government center. U.S. security cooperation is already beginning to move in this direction—for instance, with Title 22 training for QK that is not described purely as support for operations against the Islamic State.

Avoid Mirror-Imaging, Build Tactical Advantages

In general, the United States must adopt a "good enough" or "fit for purpose" mindset, which has been increasingly evident in recent U.S. "by, with, and through" operations with the Syrian Democratic Forces. The SDF case study exemplifies what Mick Mulroy and Eric Oehlerich call the "tactical advantage" model, in which the United States quickly supplements an already capable partner with just enough additional capability so that the partner can defeat current threats.[24] (Mulroy and Oehlerich contrast that model with the more expensive and slower "mirror image" model, whereby Washington seeks to exert a more lasting impact on military organization and culture by amassing new conventional armed forces according to a U.S. military template.[25]) The "tactical advantage" model discussed by Mulroy and Oehlerich describes security assistance that does not necessarily transform the partner force in any lasting way. Adopting this wise approach was a conscious decision by the Combined Joint Special Operations Task Force, which was the ideal agency to execute a thrifty "by, with, and through" campaign led by a recurring cast of U.S. special operators.[26]

In Iraq, the United States should adopt the same pragmatic approach as it did in northern Syria.[27] While NMI focuses on building institutions,

U.S. bilateral assistance should help Iraq build out intelligence-driven, direct-action capabilities in provincial-level police commando and tribal mobilization forces. This assistance would fill an important gap, requiring some procurement and training support for local special forces (e.g., for commercial-type quadcopter drones and "sub-shops," as specialized workshops are known, to do maintenance and recalibration for night vision equipment). The training can be delivered through existing CTS-run training facilities where the U.S. military has been consistently present since 2004, even during the 2012–14 period. This kind of practical and narrow assistance should also include support for ISF combat evacuation and lifesaving capabilities, plus the establishment of ISF field surgical hospitals, giving ISF members greater assurance that they will survive wounds suffered during operations.

Although the United States should, of course, encourage Iraq to operate Iraqi intelligence, surveillance, and reconnaissance and aerial strike capabilities, and the "fusion" cells required to get intelligence to strike aircraft, the United States should not be overly focused on exactly duplicating a U.S.-style ISR and surgical airstrike capability. During planned operations, the U.S. military can continue to supplement Iraqi ISR coverage using assets already committed to the Central Command theater. But more fundamentally, the ISF aspiration should not be to answer counterterrorism challenges with airstrikes inside Iraq's own territory: that response is the U.S. approach to foreign counterterrorism, but not to domestic counterterrorism in America, nor a normal end state for any country to aspire to. A more normal aspiration for Iraq will be to achieve sufficient force density to deny IS space to operate, to gain more popular support and intelligence tip-offs from the public, and to have a raiding capacity spread across all the provinces that can execute warrant-based targeting and court systems that can prosecute offenders without fear of intimidation.

Communicate Realistic Conditions and Timelines for Sustained Security Assistance

As noted in an earlier section, Washington can reasonably communicate certain expectations to the Iraqi government. The threat to U.S. forces in Iraq must reduce reasonably quickly, with particular focus on declining numbers of rocket and drone attacks. No new categories of attack—such as effective roadside bombings or counter-helicopter threats against U.S. persons—must become regular occurrences. At present, U.S. and NMI advisors are quite limited in their ability to leave their secure compounds to meet with Iraqi interlocutors and this situation must improve for security cooperation to normalize and be effective.

The risk of diversion of U.S. aid must also be reduced, meaning that Defense Ministry and CTS funding must return to higher levels, to reflect the diversion of Defense Ministry and CTS procurement and sustainment funding to the PMF. Iraq must offset this diversion and later apply any cuts to defense spending more evenly. Domestic cooperation and deconfliction between Iraqi agencies, especially with the Peshmerga, must improve meaningfully and within a short timeframe. Comprehensive integration of Kurdistan Region security forces via milestones and measures of progress is a reasonable U.S. expectation. Lastly, human rights and anti-corruption concerns must be addressed more seriously. The United States must look harder for evidence of human rights abusers and corrupt commanders within services and units that it supports. Washington should expect and review measurable progress in Iraq's weeding out of human right abusers and corrupt officers from its command cadres. If Iraq cannot demonstrate a positive trajectory on enough of those conditions, then Washington should signal its disappointment by freezing some activities, including high-profile exercises, and postponing the divestment of equipment, Peshmerga salaries, or FMF grants.

Washington must also keep a grip on other basic facts as its footprint shrinks. In 2012–14, the United States effectively "went blind" on both the growth of IS activity in Iraq and the degraded capabilities of the ISF. Going forward, America must maintain a clear and up-to-date picture of terrorist and ISF activities in Iraq. America should think creatively about how to ensure it has an accurate picture, not a mirage or a frozen snapshot. This knowledge will require inventive use of existing U.S. intelligence tools, increased use of (and support to) open-source intelligence collection systems, and a recurrent ground-sourced survey of ISF command climate, readiness, and operations that provides the same accurate view as today's Inspector General quarterly reports to Congress. As noted, U.S. advisors should, as often as practical, leave their secure compounds to go to Iraqi ministries and headquarters. Some security risk must be accepted to do this. The aim must be more engagement, with a small footprint and a lowered visual signature, putting stress on creativity and flexible operations approaches under U.S. chief of mission (ambassadorial) and NATO oversight. Ideally, U.S. advisors should be selected and promoted with consideration for their willingness to serve more than a minimum one-year period in Iraq, to aid relationship building, and to ameliorate the cycle of constant one-year reinvention of the wheel without significant incremental progress (i.e., with every new OSC-I commander deciding to "take a hard look at sustainment" but leaving before progress is banked and can be built upon).

Sketch Out "Plan B" If Normalized Security Cooperation Collapses

Earlier sections of this study have focused on the authors' base case scenario—an Iraq in which moderate political leadership continues in the 2021–25 term of government and in which the United States is neither evicted by a withdrawn invitation nor leaves because of unsustainable security risks. This view is based on detailed observation of the Iraqi scene for more than two decades, but for many observers it may still seem optimistic or even a best-case scenario. So, what if Iraq suffers setbacks that push the country in a different direction? In one scenario, the sheer volume and accuracy of militia attacks could force the cessation of all security cooperation activities and even the withdrawal of the U.S. embassy and consulate staffs in Baghdad and Erbil. What then?

Alternatively, and more damagingly, Iraq could simply disinvite foreign military advisors via a parliamentary vote that could spurs a prime minister to rescind the letter of invitation or make a decision unilateral of parliament. On January 7, 2020, the Iraqi parliament held such a session—albeit without establishing a legal quorum—at which the parties present held a vote to call for the withdrawal of all foreign forces from Iraq. Iran's militia proxies in Iraq continue to call for such a full withdrawal of all foreign forces by January 1, 2022, though today's Iraqi government has made it clear that it is not expected to occur.

A different kind of Iraqi prime minister and government might adopt a different view, though it is notable that even the Iran-leaning government of Prime Minister Adil Abdulmahdi did not take this step in the aftermath of the January 7, 2020, vote. The United States clearly has no role in picking Iraq's prime ministers, but this fundamental risk underlines the absolutely pivotal role of that office. The prime minister can make all the difference between a good U.S.-Iraq relationship and a nonexistent one. Therefore, as an obvious point, the United States should care deeply who Iraq's prime ministers are, and it should strongly support those premiers and aspiring candidates who are in favor of a continued security cooperation relationship with the U.S.-led coalition.

It is hard to overstate how devastating such a call for foreign withdrawal by the Iraqi government would be for U.S. and international presence in Iraq, and for international support to Iraq (through security cooperation, economic assistance, and investment). Perhaps even Iran's allies in Iraq would hesitate to kick away the crutches of a slowly recovering Iraqi state and society, but what if they do not? Post-Afghanistan, there should clearly be a general sharpening of thinking and a review of plans for noncombatant evacuations operations from Iraq, including Iraqi persons who are eligible, though the December 31, 2019, crisis at the U.S. embassy in Baghdad demonstrated that the system has been exercised recently and is probably in good shape. Even so, more focus must be directed to the day after such a withdrawal order so that the United States is not confronted by an outcome it has not properly prepared for. Basic questions need answering, such as the following: what does America do if an Iran-aligned government is formed under an anti-American prime minister? What steps must America take, immediately and eventually, if the coalition is disinvited? And what should Washington do if militias cause the U.S.-led coalition significant casualties in an attack?

Help Marshal the Moderate Mainstream

The first and most obvious step for Washington to clearly and starkly take is to warn Iraqi political faction leaders of the risks that may present in January 2022 and beyond. The United States should paint a realistic picture of international withdrawal from Iraq, including all its economic and diplomatic second-order impacts. Washington can help to gather a team of factions that know how to act in the case of a new effort by militias to use parliament to evict foreign forces. Such a bloc could contest any parliamentary vote, as opposed to merely abstaining from it or remaining outside the chamber. If the disinvitation is initiated at the prime ministerial level, such a bloc could marshal a parliamentary vote to demand the continuation of coalition and NATO security cooperation, and could undertake the requisite back-channel talks with all factions, including those who have historically been hostile to the U.S. presence but which may be less so today. At the same time, Washington must remain open to viable partial solutions where they are possible (such as moving some assets to the Kurdistan Region with Iraq's approval).

NATO Rebadging: A Thin Reed

Under some circumstances, NMI might be able to sustain its mission in Baghdad even after an eviction or departure of U.S. diplomatic and military presence, but only if NATO is requested by Iraq to greatly scale up its force size. This increase would probably only be possible if large numbers of U.S. personnel and systems were rebadged as NATO forces and if attacks then did not target NATO, despite an influx of U.S. personnel. In any scenario where militias have compelled a coalition withdrawal, attacks on NATO troops in Iraq are a very realistic possibility. For instance, at a major conference in Baghdad on August 31, 2021, the elder statesman of the militia factions Hadi al-Ameri said:

> We are asking that now is the time for all NATO forces to leave the country, and we support the latest agreement (Washington) that the Government made, and we will demand that the Government live up to the agreement. On the 31/12/2021 there will be no

Road Map for Future Security Cooperation

foreign forces. Nor French or Turkish—the Iraqi people are in control of their own decisions and if the French president will stay we will say no, you must leave.[28]

A sudden "on paper" transition to NMI control is thus not assured and would probably not solve the immediate problems faced by crisis scenarios, though it should be considered as an interim way to retain some influence and options for the recovery of security cooperation.

Outward-In Support via Kurdistan, Jordan, and the Gulf

In such a dire scenario, the Kurdistan Region would probably be America's least-bad plan B in Iraq. At such a moment, the United States needs to be tough-minded and stand for U.S. interests and long-term partnerships with the Kurds and Iraqi moderates. The sovereignty of Iraq is clearly a consideration, but so too is the maintenance of strategic outposts (in Syria) and strategic relationships (with Iraqi Kurdistan). If Kadhimi falls and is replaced by a pro-Iranian prime minister, the United States should not hesitate to protect its interests and its partners in Iraq using any combination of expedient measures, because Iraq will have already lost a large measure of its sovereignty to Iran.

The KRI would provide a safer environment in which certain vital aspects of the U.S. mission could be maintained even if federal Iraq became untenable as an operating area for a period of time. The Kurdistan Region is the lifeline to the coalition presence in northeast Syria. It is the base for "fly to advise" technicians supporting Iraq's aviation systems and could be used as a temporary maintenance base for Iraq's U.S.-supported aircraft. The Kurdistan Region hosts alternative command, training, and logistics hubs that could allow the continuation of security cooperation with many ISF elements or just the Peshmerga. The United States should be clear-eyed, however, that even U.S. bases in the KRI would probably face ongoing drone and rocket attacks from pro-Iran elements and Iran itself.

Turkey would ideally provide the United States with overflight access for servicing hubs in the Kurdistan Region. The United States should game out what price the Kurdistan Region and Turkey might levy to support such an ongoing presence. Fearing a growth of Iranian influence, both would probably prefer that the United States had some presence in the area, albeit a very low-profile one, giving America some potential leverage. Jordan would also offer an alternative, and thus more leverage over the Kurdistan Region and Turkey. Alongside or as a partial alternative to Kurdistan, Jordan's military bases offer some of the same potential fallback options, especially in regard to supporting the U.S. advisor mission at al-Tanf in Syria or providing a base for U.S. ISR aircraft and U.S. Special Forces training for the ISF, and exercises involving the ISF. Iraqi F-16s could potentially be maintained from Jordan's air bases also.

All these potential scenarios and their variants should be "gamed out" in classified interagency tabletop exercises. None of these workarounds would be attractive to Iraq's government and military, but Iraq must understand that they would be the remaining options if the United States either cannot or will not remain in federal Iraq. The second-order consequences of a hasty withdrawal of the U.S.-led coalition, particularly if accompanied by an eviction of NATO, need to be clearly understood by Iraqi leaders and politicians well before December 31, 2021. The departure would mean the closure of the U.S. embassy in Baghdad, and potentially other embassies, and the cessation of much of Iraq's security cooperation with Western powers plus the severe disruption of economic and humanitarian support as missions shift outside Iraq—for instance, to Jordan.

Senior foreign leader visits to Iraq would almost cease. Gulf states' support to Iraq would no doubt be largely frozen. Baghdad would cease to be a center for conferences or summits, or even for Iraqi engagement with major foreign embassies. Although these outcomes might be attractive ones for the most hardline pro-Iran militias in Iraq, the majority of Iraq's leaders have signaled that such an apocalyptic outcome is not in their interest—as in 2020 when the issue raised its head when the Trump administration threatened to withdraw the U.S. embassy from Iraq.

Notes

1   Deputy Secretary of State Wendy Sherman confirmed in a Senate hearing that the 2002 AUMF is not routinely used as the primary authority for operations in Iraq. See the U.S. Senate Hearing on Authorization for Use of Military Force (AUMF), Senate Armed Services Committee, August 31, 2021, available at https://www.c-span.org/video/?513875-1/senate-hearing-authorization-military-force-aumf.

2   "U.S. Senate Hearing on AUMF," Senate Armed Services Committee, August 31, 2021. As noted in the hearing, the United States can request new authorities if the need arises, and the president always has the right to invoke self-defense when U.S. forces are attacked, https://www.c-span.org/video/?513875-1/senate-hearing-authorization-military-force-aumf.

3   The authors would like to thank Michael Eisenstadt for his guidance over the years on the issue of unattributed attacks, which are most recently encapsulated in Michael Eisenstadt, *Operating in the Gray Zone: Countering Iran's Asymmetric Way of War*, Policy Focus 162 (Washington DC: Washington Institute, 2020), https://www.washingtoninstitute.org/policy-analysis/operating-gray-zone-countering-irans-asymmetric-way-war.

4   Coalition airstrikes in Afghanistan averaged 614 weapons releases (i.e., bombs dropped or missiles fired) per month in the year before the February 2020 Doha Agreement, compared to 233 weapons releases per month in the Operation Inherent Resolve theater (Iraq and Syria, with Syria accounting for most of the large number of weapons releases in early 2019) during the same period. As noted above, coalition kinetic support for the ISF scaled back further during 2020–21 to an average of around 7.2 airstrikes (most including multiple weapons releases) per month. This natural tapering off of the air campaign as IS targets in Iraq and Syria became increasingly scarce did not result in a significant increase in insurgent attacks, underlining both the Islamic State's weakness and the ISF's reduced reliance on coalition airpower over the last two years. The contrast with the rapid deterioration in Afghanistan after America largely discontinued direct kinetic support to the ANSF following the Doha Agreement is immediately apparent. See data at Combined Forces

Air Component Commander, "2013–2019 Airpower Statistics," U.S. Air Force, January 31, 2020, https://www.afcent.af.mil/Portals/82/Documents/Airpower%20summary/Jan%202020%20Airpower%20Summary.pdf?ver=2020-02-13-032911-670.

5 Successive Houthi offensives in Yemen's Marib province since January 2020 have only been blunted by the reengagement of Saudi airpower in Yemen. The Saudi air campaign has averaged around 109 airstrikes per month since early 2020 (the majority are frontline close air or interdiction strikes in support of Yemeni forces), after winding down during 2019 to a low of only nine strikes in December. See Yemen airstrike data at the Yemen Data Project, https://yemendataproject.org.

6 This number can be compared to twenty-four U.S. military deaths in the same period in Afghanistan. See U.S. Department of Defense, "Casualty Status as of 10 a.m. EDT September 20, 2021," available at https://www.defense.gov/casualty.pdf.

7 The Institute for Security Governance—situated within the Defense Security Cooperation University's International School of Education and Advising—is the Department of Defense's Center of Excellence for Institutional Capacity Building.

8 Iraqi Council of Representatives, "Iraq's Defense Manufacturing Law (Law No. 25 of 2019)," October 15, 2019, available at https://iraqld.hjc.iq/LoadLawBook.aspx?page=1&SC=&BookID=41818.

9 For instance, NMI arguably bounced off in its efforts to fold Iraq's five major force commands into three (by subsuming the Iraqi Army Aviation Command into the Iraqi Ground Forces Command, and similarly by trying to subsume the Iraqi Air Defense Command into the Iraqi Air Force Command. NMI also failed to merge Iraq's two military intelligence organizations into one. See Peter Dahl Thruelsen, "Misaligned in Mesopotamia: Conflicting Ambitions in NATO Mission Iraq," *War on the Rocks*, September 16, 2021, https://warontherocks.com/2021/09/misaligned-in-mesopotamia-conflicting-ambitions-in-nato-mission-iraq/.

10 Michael Knights and Wladimir van Wilgenburg, *Accidental Allies: The U.S.–Syrian Democratic Forces Partnership Against the Islamic State*, Policy Focus 168 (Washington DC: Washington Institute, 2021), https://www.washingtoninstitute.org/policy-analysis/

accidental-allies-us-syrian-democratic-forces-partnership-against-islamic-state.

11 The issue of NATO troop levels is highly sensitive in Iraq. Iraqi national security advisor Qasim al-Araji told the Rafidain Center for Dialogue Forum Baghdad 2021 that "the Government of Iraq has not yet delivered its actual demands on the number of advisors that [it] needs; [that is] why it is difficult to answer the question for the moment...the Iraqi demand is not to increase the number of advisors—that we will examine next year." See video coverage of the event at www.youtube.com/watch?v=D9AEwcaMKuc (in Arabic).

12 U.S. Department of Defense, "Joint Publication 3-22: Foreign Internal Defense," August 17, 2018, and February 2, 2021, ix, available at https://www.jcs.mil/Portals/36/Documents/Doctrine/pubs/jp3_22.pdf?ver=2018-10-10-112450-103.

13 The General Accounting Office notes: "SCOs operate under the direct authority of the Chief of Mission of the U.S. Embassy and are managed by the Geographic Combatant Command, which directs the planning and execution of security cooperation activities in alignment with DOD policies and priorities, among other things." See General Accounting Office, "Iraq: Characteristics of the Office of Security Cooperation-Iraq and How It Compares to Other DOD Security Cooperation Organizations," November 21, 2019, 2, https://www.gao.gov/assets/gao-20-196r.pdf.

14 U.S. State Department Fact Sheet, "U.S. Security Cooperation with Jordan," https://www.state.gov/u-s-security-cooperation-with-jordan/.

15 Jumana Kawar, "Jordan: U.S. Security Assistance and Border Defense Capacity Building," Middle East Institute, October 6, 2020, https://www.mei.edu/publications/jordan-us-security-assistance-and-border-defense-capacity-building.

16 U.S. State Department Fact Sheet, "U.S. Security Cooperation with Jordan," https://www.state.gov/u-s-security-cooperation-with-jordan/.

17 The United States has $4.47 billion in active government-to-government sales cases with Jordan under the Foreign Military Sales (FMS) system. Since 2016, the United States has also authorized the permanent export of more than $697 million in defense articles to Jordan via the Direct Commercial Sales process. U.S. State Department Fact Sheet, "U.S. Security Cooperation with Jordan," https://www.state.gov/u-s-security-cooperation-with-jordan/.

18 The United States has supported the Jordan Border Security Program, an integrated border security surveillance, detection, and interdiction system along 350 miles of Jordan's land borders since 2009, at a cost of more than $234 million. Kawar, "Jordan: U.S. Security Assistance," https://www.mei.edu/publications/jordan-us-security-assistance-and-border-defense-capacity-building.

19 "Washington Army National Guard Completes Jordan Rotation, Transfers Mission to the Illinois Guard," American Military News, June 16, 2020, https://americanmilitarynews.com/ai/washington-army-national-guard-completes-jordan-rotation-transfers-mission-to-the-illinois-guard/.

20 Barbara Opall-Rome, "Raytheon-Jordan Border Defense Against ISIS Enters Final Phase," Defense News, May 26, 2016, available at https://www.defensenews.com/global/mideast-africa/2016/05/26/raytheon-jordan-border-defense-against-isis-enters-final-phase/.

21 "Operation Inherent Resolve Quarterly Report, April 1–June 30, 2021," 39.

22 Since 2015, the U.S. Department of State provided Iraq with $1.25 billion in Foreign Military Financing (FMF) to improve Iraq's long-term sustainment and logistics capabilities and fund ISF professionalization. The United States has $16.3 billion in active government-to-government sales cases with Iraq under the Foreign Military Sales (FMS) system. Since 2016, the United States also authorized the permanent export of more than $689 million in defense articles to Iraq via the Direct Commercial Sales process. Iraq borrowed $3.4 billion via two FMF subsidized Credit Facility Agreements in FY2016 and FY2017, which allowed Iraq to pay for FMS purchases with borrowed funds and repay with interest over time. See U.S. State Department Fact Sheet, "U.S. Security Cooperation with Iraq," Bureau of Political-Military Affairs, July 16, 2021.

23 On May 26, 2021, the ISF deployed *quwat khasa* in multi-battalion strength at al-Muthanna Air Base in Baghdad, supported by tank units of the 9th Iraqi army division. These forces were held in readiness to intervene if militias undertook a threatened armed invasion of the government quarter, the International Zone.

24 Mick Mulroy and Eric Oehlerich, "A Tale of Two Partners: Comparing Two Approaches for Partner Force Operations," Middle East Institute,

January 29, 2020, https://www.mei.edu/publications/tale-two-partners-comparing-two-approaches-partner-force-operations.

25 Ibid.

26 The war in northeast Syria fell wholly under the Combined Joint Special Operations Task Force, and this situation shaped how the United States undertook "by, with, and through." It was a thrifty operation—with fewer economies of scale than Iraq but still cheap overall, and with far fewer U.S. personnel. There was no U.S. embassy to perform supporting actions (including effective Leahy vetting) and no large staff to make expansive plans to transform the Syrian fighters into a U.S.-style military. Knights and Wilgenburg, *Accidental Allies*, https://www.washingtoninstitute.org/policy-analysis/accidental-allies-us-syrian-democratic-forces-partnership-against-islamic-state.

27 For insights into how to better structure U.S. security cooperation to reflect Middle East social and military culture, see Michael J. Eisenstadt and Kenneth M. Pollack, "Training Better Arab Armies," *Parameters* 50, no. 3 (2020), https://press.armywarcollege.edu/parameters/vol50/iss3/10.

28 For video of the event, see Rafidain Center for Dialogue Forum Baghdad 2021, https://bit.ly/3CNHdyD.

ANNEXES

A. Categories of U.S. Security Cooperation

TITLE 10 FUNDING

Program	Objective	Controls	Authorized Amounts
§127e– Support of Special Operations to Combat Terrorism	Provide support to foreign forces, irregular forces, groups, or individuals engaged in supporting or facilitating authorized ongoing military operations by U.S. Special Operations Forces to combat terrorism.	Secretary of Defense and relevant Chief of Mission (ambassador)	Annual appropriation. Global limit of $100 million during any fiscal year.
§333– Authority to Build Capacity	Train and equip partner forces.	Defense Attaché and Office and security cooperation organizations make requests to Central Command, which makes nominations to Office of the Secretary of Defense and the Joint Staff. Defense Security Cooperation Agency provides program management and execution through the implementing agencies.	Annual appropriation. Global allocation of $1 billion per year in recent years.

TITLE 10 FUNDING

Program	Objective	Controls	Authorized Amounts
§1206 (aka 2282)– Build Counter-terrorism and Stability Operations Capacity of Foreign Military Forces	Train and equip foreign militaries to undertake counter-terrorism or stability operations.	Secretary of Defense and relevant Chief of Mission (ambassador)	Annual appropriation. Global limit of $350 million during any fiscal year.
Counter-IS Train and Equip Fund (CTEF)	Support defeat-ISIS capabilities "by, with, and through" the ISF and the vetted Syrian opposition.	Undersecretary of Defense– Comptroller, Central Command, and U.S. Army Budget Office	Annual appropriation. **$345 million requested for Iraq in FY2022.**
National Defense Authorization Act	Direct war costs of operating U.S. military forces in military operations.	Secretary of Defense	Annual appropriation. **$5.4 billion requested for Iraq and Syria in FY2022.**

TITLE 22 FUNDING

Program	Objective	Controls	Authorized Amounts
DCS–Direct Commercial Sales	U.S. government issues arms export licenses to U.S. firms through a process that includes a review for adherence to U.S. law and policy.	Department of State Bureau of Political-Military Affairs	
EDA–Excess Defense Articles	Transfers excess defense equipment to foreign governments.	U.S. military departments identify excess equipment. Central Command identifies possible recipients. Defense Security Cooperation Agency facilitates coordination and approval of requests.	Low-cost or no-cost. Paid for by recipient country national funds.
ESF–Emergency Support Fund		Department of State Bureau of Political-Military Affairs	Annual appropriation. **$150 million requested for Iraq in FY2022.**

TITLE 22 FUNDING

Program	Objective	Controls	Authorized Amounts
FMF–Foreign Military Financing	Provides grants for the acquisition of U.S. defense equipment, services, and training.	Secretary of State determines which countries will have programs. Secretary of Defense executes the program.	Annual appropriation. FMF is a source of financing and may be provided to a partner nation on either a grant (non-repayable) or direct loan basis. **$200 million requested for Iraq in FY2022.**
FMS–Foreign Military Sales	U.S. government procures U.S. defense articles as an inter-mediary for foreign partners.	Secretary of State determines which countries will have programs. Secretary of Defense executes the program.	Usually recipient country national funds.
IMET–International Military Education and Training	Provides training and education on a grant basis to students from allied and friendly nations.	Secretary of State determines which countries will have programs. Secretary of Defense executes the program.	Annual appropriation. **$1 million requested for Iraq in FY2022**.
NADR–Non-proliferation, Anti-terrorism, Demining, and Related programs	Support mine action projects by helping to develop indigenous mine action capabili-ties.	Department of State Bureau of Political-Military Affairs	Annual appropriation. **$42 million requested for Iraq in FY2022.**

B. Relative Strength of Different ISF Combat Forces

In a 2019 study, one of the authors assessed the maximum combat strength of Iran-backed Popular Mobilization Forces units as 63,000, or 83,000 if all Badr Organization forces sided with Iran-backed PMF.[1] This number compares to about 93,000 Iraqi army, CTS, and border forces, not counting any proffered aid from well over 100,000 Kurdish forces, and not counting loyalist Ministry of Interior units.[2] If Iraq remains under Iraqi nationalist leadership, with continued training and professionalization of the loyalist ISF, the military balance is likely to gradually shift against militias.

Iraqi Army

Each Iraqi army battalion has an establishment strength of 500 persons, breaking down into 20 twenty-five-person platoons. (Each company has four line platoons and one support platoon, and there are four companies to a battalion.)

There are 65 Iraqi army line brigades, including:

- 29 three-battalion brigades with an establishment strength of approximately 1,600 troops (3x500 plus 100 brigade troops [3]).
- 25 four-battalion brigades with an establishment strength of approximately 2,100 troops (4x500 plus 100 brigade troops).
- 11 three-battalion commando brigades with an establishment strength of approximately 1,600 troops (3x500 plus 100 brigade troops).
- There are 14 sets of divisional troops, which include small (250-man) divisional commando, intelligence, artillery, and engineering battalions, plus communications, logistics, and sustainment companies (support units with 250 troops). Each divisional set thus includes an establishment strength of 1,250 troops.

There are 11 sets of Operations Command (OC) troops, which include approximately 500-man force protection battalions and 1,200-man staff personnel. Ten of the OCs thus have an establishment strength of approximately 1,700 men. Baghdad Operations Command is the exception, with three supplementary reserve battalions, setting its establishment strength at approximately 3,200.

As learned from the author's interviews, Iraqi army brigades, divisional troops, and OC troops operate at 50 percent daily manning because of liberal leave policies that are intended to reduce operating costs resulting from budget shortfalls.

Formations	Establishment Strength (each)	Aggregate Establishment Strength
29 three-battalion brigades	1,600	46,400
25 four-battalion brigades	2,100	52,500
11 three-battalion commando brigades	1,600	17,600
14 sets divisional troops	1,250	17,500
10 OCs	1,700	17,000
Baghdad Operations Command	3,200	3,200
TOTAL		**154,200**
TOTAL with 50% manning		**77,100**

Ministry of Interior Federal Police

Each Federal Police battalion has an approximate establishment strength of 500 persons, breaking down into 20 twenty-five-person platoons. (Each company has four line platoons and one support platoon, and there are four companies to a battalion).

There are 31 Federal Police line brigades, including:

- 28 three-battalion brigades with an approximate establishment strength of 1,600 troops (3x500 plus 100 brigade troops[4]).
- 3 four-battalion brigades with an approximate establishment strength of 2,100 troops (4x500 plus 100 brigade troops).
- There are 7 sets of divisional troops, which include small (250-man) divisional commando, mechanized, and engineering battalions, plus communications, logistics, and sustainment companies (a support unit with 250 troops). Each divisional set thus includes an approximate establishment strength of 1,000 troops.
- As learned from the author's interviews, Federal Police brigade and divisional troops operate at 45 percent daily manning due to liberal leave policies that are intended to reduce operating costs resulting from budget shortfalls.

Formations	Establishment Strength (each)	Aggregate Establishment Strength
28 three-battalion brigades	1,600	44,800
3 four-battalion brigades	2,100	6,300
7 three-battalion commando brigades	1,000	7,000
TOTAL		**58,100**
TOTAL with 45% manning		**31,955**

Ministry of Interior Emergency Response Division

Each Emergency Response Division (ERD) battalion has an approximate establishment strength of 500 persons, breaking down into 20 twenty-five-person platoons. (Each company has four line platoons and one support platoon, and there are four companies to a battalion.)

There are 14 ERD line battalions and four sets of brigade troops, with just 100 personnel each.

As learned from the author's interviews, ERD units operate at 65 percent daily manning because of relatively good budget priority and a high operational tempo.

Formations	Establishment Strength (each)	Aggregate Establishment Strength
14 ERD line battalions	500	7,000
4 sets of ERD brigade troops	100	400
TOTAL		**7,400**
TOTAL with 65% manning		**4,810**

Ministry of Interior Emergency Police/SWAT/ Special Tactics Regiment Battalions

Each battalion has an approximate establishment strength of 350 persons.

As learned from the author's interviews, Emergency Police/SWAT/STR units operate at 40 percent daily manning because of their low operational tempo and ease of activating locally based members if needed.

Formations	Establishment Strength (each)	Aggregate Establishment Strength
122 Emergency Police/SWAT/Special Tactics Regiment battalions	350	42,700
TOTAL		42,700
TOTAL with 40% manning		17,080

Counter Terrorism Service

Each Counter Terrorism Service (CTS) battalion has an approximate establishment strength of 500 persons, breaking down into 20 twenty-five-person platoons. (Each company has four line platoons and one support platoon, and there are four companies to a battalion.)

There are 18 CTS line battalions and six sets of support and reconnaissance troops, with just 250 personnel per set.

As learned from the author's interviews, CTS units operate at 75 percent daily manning because of their very high operational tempo and the political reliance on them for key point protection missions.

Formations	Establishment Strength (each)	Aggregate Establishment Strength
18 CTS line battalions	500	9,000
6 sets of CTS sector troops	250	1,500
TOTAL		**10,500**
TOTAL with 75% manning		**7,875**

Iran-Backed (*Walai*) PMF Line Brigades

These troops include the Popular Mobilization Forces units that have strong historic loyalty ties to pro-Iran militias who support the *velayat-e faqih* (rule by the jurisprudent, as in Iran).

Most registered PMF members do not report to fielded units but instead are registered to the PMF Commission and are rarely mobilized, if at all. Fielded PMF forces use a notional brigade system, but these brigades vary enormously in size, from as few as 150 registered fighters to as many as 2,500. The average size of the brigades is (by the authors' unit-by-unit calculations) 614, making many pro-Iran PMF brigades the size of an above-strength Iraqi army battalion (i.e., one-third the size of an Iraqi army brigade).

By the authors' counting, there are 43 numbered or named Iran-backed PMF brigades, plus seven support units (each 400 persons) that lean strongly toward the *walai* camp.

As learned from the author's interviews, Iran-backed PMF brigades operate at 33 percent daily manning because of their low operational tempo, poor discipline, and the presence of a very high proportion of "ghost soldiers" in their nominal ranks.

Formations	Establishment Strength (each)	Aggregate Establishment Strength
43 line "brigades"	614	26,402
7 support units	400	2,800
TOTAL		**29,202**
TOTAL with 33% manning		**9,636**

Other (Non-*Walai*) PMF Line Brigades

These troops include the Popular Mobilization Forces units with no strong historic loyalty to pro-Iran militias who support *velayat-e faqih*. They may be Sadrist, Sunni tribal, or Atabat ("shrine units" loosely connected with the PMF and loyal to Grand Ayatollah Ali al-Sistani).

Most registered PMF members do not report to fielded units but instead are registered to the PMF Commission and are rarely mobilized, if at all. Fielded PMF forces use a notional brigade system, but these brigades vary in size, from as few as 150 registered fighters to as many as 1,000. The average size of the brigades is (by the authors' unit-by-unit calculations) 451, making many PMF (Hashd) brigades the size of an under-strength Iraqi army battalion (i.e., one quarter the size of an Iraqi army brigade).

Formations	Establishment strength (each)	Aggregate establishment strength
35 line "brigades"	451	15,798
TOTAL		**15,798**
TOTAL with 33% manning		**5,213**

Overall Comparative Personnel Levels

Without any qualitative weighting being applied, the following calculations show that the PMF—despite having an overwhelming number of registered members and checkpoint troops spread across Iraq—is remarkably out-numbered by the formal ISF. Ministry of Interior forces have the potential to balance the equation in favor of pro-Iran PMF, making the Interior Ministry key ground in the struggle to dominate Iraq's security sector.

Combat and Line Formations	Aggregate Establishment Strength	Aggregate Effective Strength
Iraqi army brigades	154,200	77,100
Federal Police brigades	58,100	31,955
Emergency Response Division	7,400	4,810
Ministry of Interior Emergency Police/ SWAT/Special Tactics Regiment battalions	42,700	17,080
Counter Terrorism Service	10,500	7,875
Walai PMF brigades	29,202	9,636
Non-*walai* PMF brigades	15,798	5,213

Note: The total PMF aggregate establishment strength for combat brigades sits far below the 135,000 billets allocated in the Iraqi budget for the PMF (with an additional 30,000 unregistered but sporadically paid volunteers also on the books, to bring the total to 165,000 maximum persons on the payroll). The difference between the 45,000 establishment strength for PMF combat brigades and the 135,000–165,000-person payroll underlines the extraordinary ratio of non-combat forces in the PMF, spread out on checkpoint networks and large numbers of duplicative—and largely unnecessary—headquarters functions.

Notes

1 Michael Knights, "Iran's Expanding Militia Army in Iraq: The New Special Groups," *CTC Sentinel* 12, no. 7 (2019), https://ctc.usma.edu/irans-expanding-militia-army-iraq-new-special-groups/.

2 Michael Knights, Hamdi Malik, and Aymenn Jawad Al-Tamimi, *Honored, Not Contained: The Future of Iraq's Popular Mobilization Forces*, Policy Focus 163 (Washington DC: Washington Institute, 2020), 135, https://www.washingtoninstitute.org/media/4125?disposition=inline.

3 The hundred or so brigade special troops include a reconnaissance platoon, a commando platoon, a maintenance platoon, and a small command staff.

4 The hundred or so brigade special troops include a reconnaissance platoon, a commando platoon, a maintenance platoon, and a small command staff.

Index

Abadi, Haider al- 2, 25
Abbasi, Abdul-Mohsen al- *27*
Abdulmahdi, Adil 25, 79
Afghanistan
    conflict with Iraq 3
    impact of self-reliance on ISF 24
    Resolute Support Mission 60
    U.S. forces in 57
    U.S. withdrawal from 9, 59
Afghan National Security Forces
    (ANSF) 2, 23
    Biden views on 23
    collapse in Kabul 5
    reliance on U.S. forces in
        Afghanistan 57
Ali, Shihab Jahid, *26*
Ameri, Hadi al- 80–81
Ameri, Saleh Nasr al- *26*
anti-American militias 5
anti-corruption 7–8, 53, 77
Araji, Ali Muhammad Salim al- *26*

backsliding 4–5, 24, 38, 48
Battat, Jaafar al- *26*
Bayati, Muhammad al- *26*
Biden, Joe 3, 23
bilateral
    OSC-I and 72–74
    programs 72–74
    relationships 15–16
    U.S.-Iraq cooperation 11, 60, 65
Bishr, Raad Mahmoud *27*
border control 29

career monitoring 63–64
coalition forces
    in Iraq 6, 8, 51, 55, 60
    in Syria 9, 58
combat operations 1, 33, 40, 41–42,
    56, 66

Combined Joint Task Force–
    Operation Inherent Resolve
    (CJTF-OIR) 1, 58, 60, 65, 72
    expiration in Iraq 12
    Iraqi-led war effort 3
    mission of 9
    NATO Mission Iraq 10
command table of ISF **26–28**
counterinsurgency 14, 29, 33, 48,
    51, 71, 73, 75
Counter–Islamic State Train and
    Equip Fund (CTEF) 12,
    38–40, 70
counterterrorism 16, 29, 76
    operations 35–36
    raids 37–38
    U.S. approach to foreign 76
Counter Terrorism Service (CTS)
    3–4, 7, 29, 38

Darraji, Jabbar Hatim al- *27*
Defense Security Cooperation
    Agency 60
Department of Border Enforcement
    32, 33, 63, 71

End-Use Monitoring program 50
equipping of Iraqi security forces
    (ISF) 39–40
European Union Advisory Mission–
    Iraq (EUAM-I) 10, 60, 62,
    69

F-16s 40–42, 82
Falahi, Mahmoud al- *28*
Fatah Alliance 2
Fayyadh, Alaa al- *26*
foreign internal defense (FID) 65–66
Foreign Military Financing (FMF)
    12, 67, 70, 72

Note: Page numbers in italics indicate figures, and page numbers in bold indicate tables.

Index

Foreign Military Sales (FMS) 12, 70, 72
Foreign Terrorist Organizations 50
fraud reduction 64
Furaiji, Ali Jassim al- *28*

"gray market" 40
"gray zone" warfare 5

Harbiyah, Saad al- *28*
Hashemi, Ali al- *28*
Hezbollah 5, 49
Hiti, Nasser Ghanim al- *27*
human resource management system 11, 63–64
human rights 7–8, 53, 77

intelligence, surveillance, and reconnaissance (ISR) 4, 16, 41–42, 58–59, 82
internal border policing, 29
international presence, 8, 17, 58–59, 79
intra-Kurdish, 7, 52–53
Iran 5
  -aligned Fatah Alliance, 2
  -backed militias 2, 8, 25, 40, *49*, 82
  Russia and, 5
Iraq
  Army Aviation Command, 37
  budget funding for security institutions *30*
  building loyalist forces within 50–51
  coalition forces in 6
  conflict with Afghanistan 3
  eviction of U.S. forces 17–18
  foreign military advisors 17
  Iraq Train and Equip Fund 38
  Ministry of Defense 14, 29
  NATO in 58
  reliance on U.S.-led forces 38–39
  security cooperation 11–12, 65, 72, 74–75
  U.S. military withdrawal from 24

Iraqi security forces (ISF) 2, 3–4, 23–43, 47–53
  backsliding 48
  clearance operations 36–37
  combat operations 41–42
  command table **26–28**
  counterterrorism operations 35–36
  design and deployment 29–31
  domestic adversaries of 5–6
  domestic primacy 49
  Iran-backed militias' risk posed to *49*
  Iraq reliance on U.S.-led forces 38–39
  leadership in 24–25
  "loyalist forces" within Iraq 50–51
  medical care systems 64
  minimal U.S. role in training, equipping, and sustaining 39–40
  monopoly of force 49
  order of battle map *32*
  personnel *31*
  rationalization and redeployment 33–35
  sustainment of air operations 40–41
  targeted counterterrorism raids 37–38
  U.S. expectations from 51–53
  victories due to U.S.-led coalition 5
Islamic State (IS) 1, 3, 9–11, 38, 48, 75
Izzi, Ghassan al- *27*

Jabbouri, Hamid al-Nams al- *27*
joint exercises 14–15
Jordan 11–12, 67–70, 81–82
Jordan Border Security Program 12
Jordanian Armed Forces 67
Jordan Operational Engagement Program (JOEP) 12, 70

Kadhimi, Mustafa al- 2, 25, 55–56

106 *Index*

Kamar, Hamid Muhammad *26*
Kenani, Talib Shaghati al- *26*
Khikhani, Nasir al- *27*
King Abdullah II Special Operations
　　Training Center (KASOTC)
　　14, 73
Kurdistan 81–82
Kurdistan Control Line (KCL) 13, 33,
　　34, 35
Kurdistan Democratic Party (KDP) 53
Kurdistan Region of Iraq (KRI) 7, 19,
　　25, 29, 33, 35, 81

law enforcement, rural 29
leadership
　　Iraqi 39
　　in Iraqi security forces (ISF) 24–25
　　military 5, 48
　　political 2, 17
　　quality of 25
Lockheed Martin 40
logistics management 63

Mahlawi, Ismail Shibab al- *28*
Majidi, Ali al- *28*
Maliki, Nazzal al- *28*
Maliki, Nouri al- 24
Mashgal, Ali *27*
medical care systems 64
Military Advisory Group (MAG) 59
military education 63, 67
Ministry of Defense (Iraq) 7, 14, 29,
　　52, 62, 73
Ministry of Interior (Iraq) 29, 49–50,
　　62
monopoly of force 49
Muhammadawi, Qais al- *27*
Mulroy, Mick 75
Musawi, Thiya al- *26*
Mustafa, Salahuddin *26*

National Defense Strategy 62
National Security Strategy 62
NATO 60–65, *61*
　　capacity building of 9–11
　　expansion of 64–65

in Iraq 58
rebadging 80–81
NATO Mission Iraq (NMI) 9–10, 60,
　　73
　　Defense Ministry 63
　　effectiveness of 11, 62
non-combat support 41–42

Obama, Barack 3
Obeid, Jabbar *26*
Oehlerich, Eric 75
Office of Security Cooperation–Iraq
　　(OSC-I) 62, 63, 72–74, 78
off-ramp for former soldiers 64
Operation Inherent Resolve 51
Operations Commands (OCs) 25, 36

Patriotic Union of Kurdistan (PUK) 53
performance monitoring 63–64
Persian Gulf 81–82
Popular Mobilization Forces (PMF)
　　5, 7, 25, 29, 48, 64
professional military education 63,
　　67

rationalization in ISF 33–35
readiness initiatives 11
readiness workshops 63
redeployment in ISF 33–35
rural law enforcement 29

Saadi, Abdul-Wahab al- *26*
Saadi, Maan al-, *26*
Saddam, Akram, *28*
security cooperation 6–8, 55–82
　　bilateral programs 72–74
　　developing multiyear 70–71
　　foreign internal defense (FID)
　　　65–66
　　international presence 58–59
　　in Iraq *68*
　　Jordan 67–70, 81–82
　　Kurdistan 81–82
　　NATO 60–65, *61*, 80–81
　　Persian Gulf 81–82
　　plan 13–14

plan B in case of collapse 78–79
risks of full withdrawal 57–58
sustained security assistance
76–78
tactical advantage 75–76
U.S.-led military safety net
55–57
Security Sector Reform Trust Fund
71
security threat 51–52
to U.S. advisors 6
Shia 35
Special Operations Advisor Group
38
structure planning 11, 62
Sunni(s) 35
sustained security assistance 76–78
Syria 8, 9
coalition forces in 58
Syrian Democratic Forces (SDF) 16,
75

tactical advantage 16, 75–76
Tai, Jabbar Naima al- *28*
Tamimi, Karim al- *26*
temporary plan B 18–19
training
CTS-run 76
Iraqi security forces (ISF) 39–40
syllabi 63
U.S. Special Forces 19
via joint exercises 14–15

Trump, Donald 3, 82

UN Development Programme 10, 60
United States
international diplomatic
presence and 57–58
Iraq and 74–75
military safety net 55–57
risk of diversion of aid offered by
7, 52
security cooperation 6–8
urban law enforcement 29
U.S. Air Tasking Order 41
U.S. Congress 2, 36, 40, 42, 67, 74,
78
U.S. Counter-IS Train and Equip
Fund 73
U.S. International Organization for
Migration 62
U.S.-Jordan Defense Cooperation
Agreement 15, 74
U.S. Special Forces 82
U.S. Title 10 *68*
U.S. Title 22 *68*
U.S. Title 50 *68*
Utaibi, Ahmed Salim Bahjat al- *27*

Yarallah, Abdul-Amir *26*

Zaidi, Abdul-Amir al- *26*
Zaki, Samir *26*
Zuhairi, Hamid al- *27*